TASTE OF BROADWAY

RESTAURANT RECIPES FROM NYC'S THEATER DISTRICT

CARLISS RETIF POND

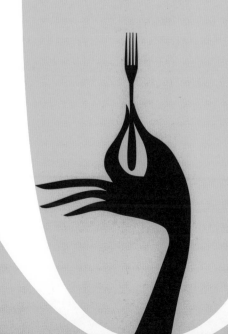

GIBBS SMITH
TO ENRICH AND INSPIRE HUMANKIND

First Edition
14 13 12 11 10   5 4 3 2 1

Text © 2010 Carliss Retif Pond
Photographs © 2010 Jess Espinosa

Published by
Gibbs Smith
P.O. Box 667
Layton, Utah 84041

1.800.835.4993 orders
www.gibbs-smith.com

Designed by Debra McQuiston
Printed and bound in China
Gibbs Smith books are printed on either recycled, 100% post-consumer
waste. FSC-certified papers or on paper produced from a 100% certified
sustainable forest/controlled wood source.

Library of Congress Cataloging-in-Publication Data
Pond. Carliss Retif.
  Taste of Broadway : restaurant recipes from NYC's Theater District /
Carliss Pond. — 1st ed.
      p. cm.
  ISBN-13: 978-1-4236-0486-0
  ISBN-10: 1-4236-0486-5
  1. Cookery. International. 2. Restaurants—New York (State)—New
York. I. Title.
  TX725.A1P646 2010
  641.59747—dc22
                        2009035221

NEW
Applebee's
Times Square Starts Here!
BUS LANE
TOW & FINE
Hilton
WINNER

conten

ts

"My husband Jerry was the quintessential New Yorker. Everyone knew him for his many Broadway shows and *Law & Order*, but our neighbors knew him as the guy who lives on 8th and 53rd. They have since renamed that intersection in his honor, Jerry Orbach Way. We rarely left the Hell's Kitchen and Theater District neighborhoods, and Jerry was always seen at the corner pizza place, hot dog stand, and deli. Yes, he was a theater and TV star but, in his mind, he was 'that regular guy.'"

—Elaine Cancilla Orbach, former Broadway dancer

introduction

New York City's famous Theater District, also widely known as Broadway or the "Great White Way," is one of the most popular tourist attractions in the world, luring millions every year. While the show is the "thing," the evening becomes an event in itself with a pre-theater or post-theater dinner in one of the myriad restaurants in the area. From century-old institutions continuing the "old New York" tradition to the newer innovative restaurants beginning their own traditions, the choices offer tastes for every palate and budget. Whether it's a mile-high pastrami sandwich from the corner deli or succulent jumbo lump crabcakes at an upscale establishment, the experience is always quintessential New York.

Commonly thought of as just a tourist attraction, the Theater District is also a neighborhood whose residents are regulars at many of these establishments. People from all walks of life eat, drink, and mingle on a daily basis, giving the area its sense of community. The two groups—tourists and locals—demand an abundance and variety of eating places.

Restaurants, cafes, diners, and delis not only serve up some of the most delicious food in the world but also offer characters and stories as colorful and dramatic as those onstage. As customers "people watch" in amazement, it is quite common to hear the waiter or waitress say, "Not to worry, no charge for the entertainment." It's truly one of the best deals in town!

One of New York's most famous institutions is Sardi's, well known for the show-biz caricatures that grace the walls. What many don't realize is that it is still family owned and operated. Sean Rickett, the great-grandson of Vincent Sardi Sr., is regularly seen at the door greeting patrons, as did his grandfather and great-grandfather before him. The original eatery, The Little Restaurant, opened in 1921 but moved down the street to its present location in 1927 when the Shubert brothers offered them space in their newly constructed building. A marriage made in heaven!

Another family restaurant, Pergola Des Artistes (Arbor or Shelter for Artists) has survived and thrived since 1962 following countless setbacks. Marie and Jacques Ponsolle, speaking no English, came to New York City from a tiny town in France. Working long hours in kitchens, they saved and eventually opened their own restaurant. The first week: no customers, robbed of the $40 in the register, and a basement flood that ruined all food and removed all wine labels. The determined couple glued the labels back on. Today, Marie continues to work in her cozy, popular French restaurant with her sons, Christian and Laurent, and grandson Christopher. Truly an example of how "the show must go on."

For over a hundred years, the Algonquin has welcomed actors, playwrights, literary figures, journalists and more. But probably the most famous is Matilda, a resident of the hotel since the 1930s. It was then that a shabby cat entered, meowing for food. Always priding himself on service and hospitality, owner Frank Case welcomed her, and there has been a Matilda running the establishment ever since. As the New York celebrity that she is, Matilda has a birthday party every year. In 2002, perhaps feeling more a diva than ever surrounded by 150 of her closest friends,

she jumped in her birthday cake. The chef rose to the occasion and no guest left without dessert. You can see this feline star at www. algonquinhotel.com or email her directly at matildaalgonquin@algonquin.com.

Ol' Blue Eyes! Does anyone need more information than that? Say "Patsy's in Manhattan" and the immediate response is, "Oh, Frank Sinatra's hangout!" Founded in 1944 by Pasquale "Patsy" Scognamillo, this quintessential Italian restaurant has had only three chefs: Patsy himself, his son Joe, and grandson Sal. Some believe that Frank's ghost still visits his old haunt to indulge in his favorites dishes. Even if you don't believe in ghosts, you might find yourself sitting next to George Clooney, Al Pacino, Placido Domingo, or Robert DeNiro. An extra treat at no extra charge.

At the turn of the twentieth century, Alan Rosen's great-grandparents lived in a New York tenement after emigrating from the Ukraine. His grandmother saved every penny and bought a share in a luncheonette for two of her sons, Harry, sixteen, and Mike, eighteen, where they became known for their sandwiches and sodas. It was the beginning of the Rosen tradition, and today Alan continues the family business in Shubert Alley, serving up "the best cheesecake in New York City."

One of the Theater District's most popular steakhouses is Frankie & Johnnie's, which opened in 1926 as a speakeasy at the height of Prohibition. Patrons would knock on an unmarked door and a tiny peephole would open. The person on the outside would whisper "Frankie," and if the reply was "Johnnie," it meant a night of drinking, eating, and frolicking.

"For two decades, I have tended bar at one of New York City's most famous institutions. During that time, I've watched star-struck tourists timidly enter, intrigued with the mystique. But when they leave, the mystique disappears. What they experience is a family-owned restaurant frequented by celebrities who leave their characters in the theaters and become 'real people.' And out-of-towners return home feeling they have been adopted into an extended family. That's one of the many reasons I love my job."

—Jose Estevez, bartender, Sardi's

Another Prohibition-era speakeasy, now a restaurant, that has been frequented by countless movie stars, theater figures, and presidents throughout the decades is '21' Club, commonly referred to as '21'. The distinct facade sports twenty-one painted cast-iron jockey statues along the building's ornate balcony. Scenes from some of the most popular movies and television shows are set here, including *Breakfast at Tiffany's*, *All About Eve*, *Wall Street*, *I Love Lucy*, and *Sex and the City*. The club's vault, or wine cellar, holds private wine collections of many celebrities', and you can ask to see it.

Many people assume that Broadway Joe and this Steak House belong to Joe Namath, the New York Jets football superstar of the 1970s. Although his photo hangs on the bar wall and he was a regular, Namath was not the owner. Joe Moreno opened this restaurant over fifty years ago, and it became a hotspot for the theater group as a popular site for movie shoots, including *FBI Story* with James Stewart and *Sweet Charity* with Shirley MacLaine. Check out the great mural wall and see if you recognize anyone.

Anyone who has ever seen Dustin Hoffman in *Tootsie* will never forget that scene of him decked out in the bright red sequined dress, sitting in the ornate gold and red Russian Tea Room. A classic movie in a classic NYC restaurant! While not originally a "glamour" destination, the tea room was opened in 1927 by former members of the Russian Imperial ballet and quickly became the safe haven for Russian expatriates. Today, the decor might be more elaborate, but it still remains a safe haven for all those in the entertainment industry. To find your way there, just remember "six minutes and twenty-three seconds from Lincoln Center and slightly to the left of Carnegie Hall."

If directions are your strong point but watching the clock is not, there is a perfect place for you. As I always say, "The Theater District neighborhood will take care of all your concerns." Head to the Hourglass Tavern for great food in a family environment—and there is an hourglass at each table. When you receive your order, the waiter turns the hourglass and you know exactly how much time is left before the curtain goes up. Let the hourglass work. Relax, don't rush, don't think, just enjoy a great dinner, and show. Even the Big Apple slows its pace!

Applause is well deserved for all culinary stars who have created and continue to create the Theater District food delights. The theater has its chorus lines, stage hands, and understudies, while the food industry has its waiters, waitresses, and bartenders. Ask any of the gracious servers what they do and the answer will be overwhelmingly, "I'm an actor!" "I'm a dancer!" "I'm a singer!" "I'm a playwright!" And it is always said with unwavering youthful enthusiasm and belief.

Countless times, I have sat in a restaurant or diner listening to parents plead with their child to "come home" because "it's impossible to make it here and, besides, it's too dangerous in this city." I eavesdrop, knowing the response will always be the same: "No, I know I can make it!" Some do, but regardless, they at least experience the passion and energy of Broadway. And no one can ever take that away from them.

Enjoy this taste of Broadway. Entertainment and entertainers are everywhere!

starters

Marie's Chicken Livers

Pergola Des Artistes, courtesy of Jean-Christian Ponsolle

3 tablespoons olive oil, divided
1 (10-ounce) package fresh
    cremini mushrooms, sliced
1/2 teaspoon fresh thyme, divided
Salt and pepper to taste

1 small onion, finely chopped
1 pound chicken livers
1/2 cup dry sherry
1 French baguette, sliced

SERVES 4

In a large skillet, heat 1 tablespoon oil over medium heat. Add mushrooms and cook until softened and browned, about 8–10 minutes. Add 1/4 teaspoon thyme, salt, and pepper and set aside in a small mixing bowl.

In the same skillet, heat another tablespoon oil. Add onion and sauté until light brown. Add remaining thyme and season with salt and pepper. Add to the mushroom bowl and toss lightly.

In the same skillet, heat remaining olive oil over medium heat. Add chicken livers and sauté until browned, about 4–5 minutes. Increase heat to medium-high, add sherry and cook about 8–10 minutes. Reduce heat, add the mushroom mixture, and simmer about 8–10 minutes. Serve with the sliced baguette.

It is hard to believe that this delectable dish has no butter or cream. The secret—and a great advantage—is that it can be prepared a day ahead of time. When it is gently reheated, it takes on a delicious velvety texture that will delight even those who have disliked liver in the past.

Crabmeat-Stuffed Avocado

**Broadway Joe Steakhouse,
courtesy of Luciano Marchignoli**

2 ripe avocados
1 plum tomato, small dice
1 serrano pepper, minced
½ cup crabmeat
⅛ cup finely chopped onion

Juice of 1 lemon
Splash of tequila
Pepper to taste
4 large cooked shrimp to garnish
Mixed baby greens (optional)

SERVES 4

Cut avocados in half and carefully scoop out the pulp into a
bowl, reserving the skins. Mash avocado and gently fold in
remaining ingredients except shrimp and baby greens. Divide
mixture into the 4 avocado skins and top each with 1 shrimp.
Serve on a bed of baby greens, if desired.

A double delight happens when succulent
shrimp and crabmeat come together and complement the buttery flavor of the avocado. With
just a touch of tequila, this appetizer transports
one to the Mexican Riviera.

Sea Scallops with Lemon Thyme, Mint, and Tomato Sauce

Algonquin Hotel, courtesy of Alex Aubrey

TOMATO SAUCE

2 tablespoons olive oil

2 cloves garlic, minced

¼ cup finely chopped onion

2 cups canned diced tomatoes

Salt and pepper to taste

SCALLOPS

8 sea scallops, scored

Olive oil

2 tablespoons fresh mint, cut
   in thin strips to garnish

1 tablespoon lemon thyme leaves to garnish

SERVES 4

In a heavy saucepan, heat the oil over medium-high heat. Add garlic and onion and sauté for 2–3 minutes. Add the tomatoes, bring to a boil, reduce heat to low, and simmer for 8–10 minutes. Season to taste with salt and pepper.

Lightly brush scallops with oil and season with salt and pepper. In a large nonstick skillet, sear scallops over medium-high heat for 2 minutes on each side.

Divide the tomato sauce among appetizer plates and top with 2 scallops each. Garnish with the mint and lemon thyme leaves.

Lemon thyme, a variety of wild thyme, adds a delightful lemon aroma and perfect zip to these quickly seared sweet and moist large scallops.

Chorizo al Vino Tinto

Meson Sevilla, courtesy of Joaquin Lucero

4 Spanish chorizo sausages (do
   not substitute Mexican)
Spanish red table wine to cover sausages

¼ cup extra virgin olive oil
1 cup chopped onion

SERVES 4

Place sausage links in a large, heavy, deep skillet and cover
with red wine. Bring to a boil, reduce heat, and simmer for 20
minutes. Remove sausage and set aside to cool. Reserve wine,
separately, on the side. When chorizo is cool, cut on an angle
into ¼-inch slices.

In the same skillet, heat the oil over medium heat. Add the
onion and sauté until transparent. Return chorizo slices to the
skillet and sauté until slightly browned. Add reserved wine and
cook over medium heat until reduced. Serve piping hot with
warm, crusty bread.

This pork sausage spiced with garlic and chili
powder is taken to new heights when simmered
in red wine. There is a difference between Spanish and Mexican chorizo: Spanish is made with
smoked pork, while Mexican contains fresh.

Black plantains are intensely sweet while yellow ones are mildly sweet, which makes the yellow ones perfect for this savory dish. They add just the hint of sweetness to the pork and spices.

Bartolito

Victor's Café, courtesy of Fernando Marulanda

PICADILLO
2 tablespoons canola oil

1/3 cup chopped onion

2 cloves garlic, minced

1/2 pound chopped pork

1–2 teaspoons ground cumin

1–2 teaspoons dried oregano

1 tablespoon white vinegar

1/2 cup chopped tomatoes

1 teaspoon chicken base

1 teaspoon beef base

2 tablespoons chopped raisins

1 tablespoon ketchup

MASA DE PLATANO
2 yellow plantains, unpeeled
   and ends cut off

Olive oil

Salt

Canola oil for frying

SERVES 4

In a large, heavy skillet, heat canola oil over medium-high heat. Add onion and garlic and sauté until transparent. Add the pork, cumin and oregano and cook until browned. Stir in the vinegar, tomatoes, chicken base, beef base, and raisins. Cook until most of the liquid has evaporated and then thoroughly blend in ketchup. Set aside to cool.

In a large pot, boil the plantains in salted water until the skins break and the plantains are tender. Drain and allow to cool.

In a food processor, puree the plantains, drizzling with olive oil, until they reach a mashed consistency. Season to taste with salt.

Line four (6-ounce and 2 inch-high) ramekins with plastic wrap. Divide half of the plantain mash among the ramekins, covering the bottoms and sides. In the center of each, place one-fourth of the picadillo. Cover with the remaining plantain mash.

In a large, heavy skillet, heat 1 inch canola oil over medium-high heat. Carefully remove bartolitos from ramekins and fry until golden brown, about 2–3 minutes on each side.

Shrimp Scampi

Patsy's, courtesy of Sal Scognamillo

4 tablespoons unsalted butter
8 cloves garlic, minced
16 jumbo shrimp, peeled and deveined
Juice of 2 lemons
¼ cup clam juice
1 teaspoon Worcestershire sauce

1 teaspoon paprika
Salt and freshly ground pepper to taste
¼–⅓ cup Italian seasoned breadcrumbs
2–3 tablespoons extra virgin olive oil
Lemon wedges to garnish

SERVES 4

Preheat the broiler.

In a large, heavy, ovenproof skillet, melt the butter on low heat. Add the garlic and sauté until golden brown, about 2–3 minutes. Add the shrimp and cook for 1–2 minutes, stirring well to coat the shrimp. Stir in the lemon juice, clam juice, and Worcestershire sauce and bring to a boil. Cover, reduce heat, and simmer for 1–2 minutes. Remove cover, sprinkle the shrimp with paprika, salt and pepper and place under the broiler for 5–6 minutes, or until shrimp are cooked and lightly browned. Remove from oven, sprinkle with breadcrumbs and drizzle with oil. Place under broiler until breadcrumbs are lightly browned, about 2–3 minutes. Serve immediately with lemon wedges and crusty bread.

This dish has been a favorite for generations. *Scampi,* Italian for tiny lobsters, is substituted in America with jumbo shrimp. So, basically, this dish combines Italian techniques with American ingredients.

Ravioli Dopo Teatro

Trattoria Dopo Teatro, courtesy of Roberto Lamonte

4 uncooked lasagna strips
¼ cup olive oil
2 cloves garlic, minced
2 cups cooked lobster meat
2 tablespoons finely chopped

Italian parsley
1 cup dry white wine
1 cup tomato sauce
Salt and pepper to taste
¼ cup chopped Italian parsley to garnish

SERVES 4

Cook lasagna strips according to package directions.

Heat the oil in a large, heavy skillet over medium-high heat and sauté the garlic until lightly browned. Set aside and cool for 1 minute. Return to heat, add lobster and parsley and cook for 5 minutes, stirring gently. Add the white wine and cook over medium heat until wine evaporates. Stir in the tomato sauce, salt, and pepper and simmer about 4–5 minutes.

Drain the cooked lasagna strips and cut each in half. Place a half strip on each plate, top with one-fourth of the lobster mixture and another half strip. Sprinkle with chopped parsley and serve.

This ravioli has a twist that takes the work out of the process. There is no tedious labor of filling little pockets of dough. Instead, luscious lobster filling is placed between lasagna strips, creating the ultimate easy-elegance appetizer.

Smoked Trout and Fingerling Potato Cakes

'21' Club, courtesy of John Greeley

LEMON-CHIVE EMULSION
¾ cup mayonnaise
¼ cup olive oil
Juice and zest from 1 lemon
1 tablespoon chopped parsley
1 tablespoon chopped fresh chives

POTATO CAKES
¼ cup olive oil
2 tablespoons finely chopped onion
2 tablespoons finely chopped
   leek, white part only
2 tablespoons finely chopped celery

SERVES 4

Thoroughly mix all emulsion ingredients in a nonreactive bowl and chill in the refrigerator.

In a large, heavy skillet, heat the oil over medium heat. Add onion, leek, and celery and cook until transparent, about 3–4 minutes. Cool.

In a large nonreactive bowl, fold together the sautéed mixture, potatoes, trout, egg yolk, herbs and spice blend. Divide into 4 balls and gently flatten to form small cakes.

Probably the most popular vegetable around the world, this thumb-size variety of potato is blended with smoked trout and fried to create the ultimate potato cake. The light lemon-chive dressing is the perfect accent.

1 cup peeled, cooked, and crushed
   fingerling potatoes, cooled
½ cup cooked potato puree (1
   Yukon gold potato, boiled, cooled,
   and pureed through ricer)
1 cup flaked boneless smoked trout
1 egg yolk

1 teaspoon each chopped fresh
   chives, parsley, and tarragon
1 teaspoon salt and pepper, or to taste
2 cups flour
4 eggs, beaten with 2 tablespoons water
2 cups panko breadcrumbs
Canola oil for sautéing
Fried parsnip crisps and fresh
   watercress to garnish (optional)

Coat each cake in flour, dip in egg wash, and then coat with panko.

In the skillet, heat about ½ inch canola oil over medium heat. Sauté the potato cakes until light golden brown, about 3–4 minutes on each side. Serve with the emulsion and garnish with parsnip crisps and watercress.

"Audience members, and even students of the theater, can really identify with an actor onstage. When Ralph Fiennes performed Hamlet on Broadway, one of my theatrical friends was so nervous for his favorite actor at the premiere that he could not eat dinner before the performance. This kind of identification with a particular performer makes many people question the sanity of some audience members, but this example reminds me of the power of theater."

—John DiGaetani, professor of English and drama, New York and London

Chicken Satay

Ellen's Stardust Diner, courtesy of Brian Heyman

2 (6–8-ounce) chicken breasts
2 tablespoons olive oil
Salt and pepper to taste
12 wooden skewers, soaked
in water for 1 hour

1 cup teriyaki glaze, heated over low heat
¼ cup black and white sesame seeds
Lettuce leaves and lime wedges to garnish

SERVES 4

Gently pound chicken breasts to a uniform thickness and then cut each into 6 strips. Brush with oil and season with salt and pepper. Weave each strip on a wooden skewer.

Heat a stovetop grill over medium heat and grill chicken until seared, about 3–5 minutes on each side. When chicken is done, coat generously with the warm teriyaki and sprinkle with sesame seeds. Serve on a bed of lettuce with lime wedges.

This version of Indonesia's popular national dish cuts preparation time but doesn't cut flavor. Rather than being marinated, the chicken is cooked and then quickly glazed with teriyaki sauce and sprinkled with black and white sesame seeds.

Pan con Tomate

Sangria 46, courtesy of Benny Castro

4 ripe tomatoes
4 large cloves garlic, crushed
   in a mortar and pestle
Extra virgin olive oil
Salt and freshly ground pepper to taste

1 loaf rustic-style bread, 4–5
   inches in diameter
Jamón Serrano, Queso Manchego, or
   Chorizo Cantimpalo (optional)

SERVES 4

Puree the tomatoes by rubbing on the coarse side of a cheese grater. Place in a bowl and thoroughly mix in the crushed garlic. Drizzle in the oil until a chunky consistency is reached, but do not over oil. Season with salt and pepper.

Cut bread into 1½- to 2-inch slices and toast on both sides. Spread with tomato blend and add toppings, if using. Serve.

Rustic bread is topped with fresh garlic and tomato spread and then drizzled with extra virgin olive oil. Delicious eaten alone, it may also be topped with your favorite, ham, cheese, or sausage.

Stuffed Clams

Maison, courtesy of Mario Urgiles

1 cup panko breadcrumbs

4 tablespoons chopped parsley, divided

1/2 cup dry white wine

1/2 cup clarified butter

2 sticks unsalted butter

Salt and pepper to taste

12 top neck clams

Lemon wedges to garnish

SERVES 6

Preheat oven to 350 degrees F.

In a small bowl, mix the panko, 2 tablespoons parsley, white wine, and clarified butter and set aside.

With a hand mixer, beat the butter, remaining parsley, salt, and pepper until smooth. Spread evenly on top of the clams and then sprinkle tops with the panko mixture. Bake about 4–5 minutes. Place under the broiler for 1–2 minutes, or until crispy. Serve with lemon wedges.

Top neck clams are quahog large, round, hard-shelled clams and there are roughly four clams to a pound. Here they are simply combined with panko, white wine, and clarified butter and baked to bring out their delicate flavor.

Portobello Ole

Sangria 46, courtesy of Benny Castro

4 portobello mushrooms
1 cup olive oil
3 cloves garlic, coarsely chopped
4 strips smoked salmon

4 (¼-inch) slices Manchego cheese,
    large enough to cover the portobellos
Freshly ground pepper

SERVES 4

In a nonreactive dish, marinate the mushrooms in the oil and garlic for 1 hour, turning every 15 minutes. Reserve marinade and place mushrooms on a baking sheet; broil 4–5 inches from the heat for 45–60 seconds on each side, or until browned. Remove from broiler, and put salmon strips on upside-down mushrooms. Broil 1–2 minutes and remove from oven. Cover the salmon and mushrooms with the cheese, drizzle with reserved oil and sprinkle with pepper. Broil again until the cheese melts, about 1–2 minutes. Carefully watch the broiling process throughout to avoid burning.

Popular in the Canary Islands, this dish is a wonderful combination of both island and inland cuisine. It is substantial enough to be served as a meal in itself along with a crisp green salad.

Eggplant Involtino

Basso56, courtesy of Paolo Marco

3 large eggplants
Salt and pepper to taste
Olive oil

PESTO
3 cups loosely packed basil
   leaves, stems discarded
6 tablespoons olive oil

2 cloves garlic, chopped
2 tablespoons pine nuts
½ cup goat cheese
2 tablespoons grated Parmesan cheese
½ cup chicken or vegetable stock
⅓ cup shredded basil leaves
8 cherry tomatoes, halved

SERVES 4

Slice eggplant lengthwise in ⅛-inch strips until the seeds are reached. (A mandoline is useful here.) Turn the eggplant and do the same to the other side, discarding the part with seeds. Season the eggplant with salt and pepper and lightly brush with oil.

On a stovetop grill over medium-high heat, grill the eggplant strips 1–2 minutes on each side until lightly browned. Set aside.

In a food processor, puree the basil, oil, garlic, and pine nuts until smooth.

In a bowl, combine the pesto with the goat cheese and Parmesan cheese. Spread each eggplant strip with a thin layer of the pesto mixture and roll. Place on a baking sheet and refrigerate for 30 minutes.

Preheat oven to 375 degrees. Place the basil leaves, tomatoes, and stock around the rolls and then bake for 5 minutes.

Catini Involtino is an Italian roulade made of thinly sliced meat or vegetable that is filled, rolled, and baked. Here, pesto is rolled in thin slices of eggplant and baked for a short time, making it a quick but delicious beginning to any meal.

"Of all the Theater District eateries I haunted during the late '70s to the early '90s, one stands out most in my memory. The long-gone Jimmy Ray's, a popular destination for scoreless Broadway entertainers on 8th Avenue, served the tastiest burgers I have ever had. Maybe it was the way a beer and burger felt after a long night's work at the Comedy Club, or maybe the burgers really were magical. Served on an English muffin with Dijon mustard and never burger-friendly Heinz! No one knew why, but it worked.

"Heady times, they were. I wonder what new memories the Theater District restaurants are cooking up these days. Only time will tell."

—Eliot Camaren, writer and copublisher, *Clinton Chronicle: The Newspaper of Record for Hell's Kitchen & Midtown West*

NIKAS
GOLDEN D BRAND
Brooklyn, N.Y. 11211
THE AL HIR
"It's impossi

Ultimate Crabcakes, with Cucumber, California Olive, and Red Onion Salad

Lucille's Grill at B.B. King, courtesy of Master Chef Erik Blauberg

2 tablespoons vegetable oil

1 tablespoon minced jalapeño, skin and seeds removed

½ cup minced red bell pepper, skin and seeds removed

¼ cup minced onions

Sea salt and freshly ground black pepper to taste

2 egg yolks

1 tablespoon Tabasco sauce

2 tablespoons fresh lime juice

5 tablespoons mayonnaise

1 tablespoon chopped chives

½ tablespoon finely chopped flat-leaf parsley

2 teaspoons finely chopped cilantro

Pinch of cayenne pepper

½ pound jumbo lump crabmeat

½ cup soft breadcrumbs

¼ cup panko breadcrumbs

SERVES 4

In a large, heavy skillet, heat oil over medium-low heat. Add the jalapeño, bell pepper, onion, salt, and pepper. Sweat the vegetables until transparent, about 5 minutes. Remove from heat and cool. Place the vegetables in a mixing bowl and stir in the egg yolks, Tabasco, and lime juice. Fold in the mayonnaise, chives, parsley, cilantro, and cayenne pepper. Gently fold in the crabmeat and stir. Lightly mix in the breadcrumbs and panko so as not to break up the crabmeat. Adjust seasoning with salt and pepper. Shape the crabmeat into 4 patties.

Delicate and luscious jumbo crabmeat is gently combined with fresh herbs and vegetables and then lightly sautéed. Served with a salad of mild, crisp cucumbers, fresh dill, and lime juice, these crabcakes make the perfect spring or summer starter.

¼ cup vegetable oil
3 lemon thyme sprigs
1 teaspoon unsalted butter
½ cup micro arugula

SALAD
2 cucumbers, peeled, seeded,
  and thinly sliced

1 red onion, thinly sliced
½ cup thinly sliced California green olives
¼ cup chopped dill
½ cup olive oil
Juice from 2 limes
2 tablespoons thinly sliced scallions
2 tablespoons chopped parsley
Sea salt and freshly ground pepper to taste

At this point, make the salad. In a large mixing bowl, combine all salad ingredients and toss lightly.

In a heavy skillet, heat the oil over medium heat.

Carefully place the patties in the pan and cook slowly for 3½ minutes. Turn the patties and add the thyme sprigs and butter and cook for 3½ minutes, while continually basting.

Divide the salad in the center of four plates and top with a crab cake. Garnish with the micro arugula and serve immediately.

salads

Tabbouleh

Joe Allen, courtesy of Victor Flores

2 cups organic bulgar wheat
4 cups boiling water
2 cups ½-inch diced plum tomatoes
1 cup finely chopped Italian parsley
½ cup chopped red onion
½ cup chopped niçoise olives

DRESSING

1 cup extra virgin olive oil
½ cup chopped fresh mint leaves
¼ cup white or red wine vinegar
Salt and pepper to taste

SERVES 4–6

Place bulgar wheat in a large bowl and pour boiling water over it. Cover with plastic wrap and set aside for 2 hours.

In a blender, mix all dressing ingredients until emulsified; set aside.

When bulgar is ready, fold in tomatoes, parsley, onion, and olives. Add dressing gradually to achieve desired taste. Serve at room temperature.

This refreshing Middle Eastern salad of bulgar, mint, and fresh tomatoes is not only delicious but also healthy. Ripe French niçoise olives add a delightful taste to this salad that can also be part of a meze (hors d'oeuvres) table.

Channa Chat

Purnima, courtesy of Vikas Khanna

4 cups canned garbanzo beans,
   rinsed and drained
1 tablespoon tamarind paste
   or juice of 1 lemon
1 teaspoon cumin seeds,

   roasted and ground
¾ cup chopped red onion
2 fresh serrano peppers, seeded
   and finely chopped
2 tablespoons finely chopped fresh cilantro

SERVES 4

In a nonreactive serving bowl, toss all ingredients until well blended. Serve at room temperature.

Tamarind paste can be found in ethnic groceries and in some supermarkets and is worth the effort to seek out. It acts as a souring agent and gives this salad an added zip.

Arugula con Gamberetti

Lattanzi, courtesy of Carla Lattanzi

6 tablespoons olive oil
3 tablespoons balsamic vinegar
Salt and pepper to taste

1 pound cooked baby shrimp,
   without shells
4–6 cups baby arugula

SERVES 4

Whisk together the oil, vinegar, salt, and pepper. Add shrimp, coat well, and marinate for 30 minutes. Add arugula to shrimp and toss well. Season to taste with salt and pepper. Serve family style on a large, flat dish.

Baby arugula and baby shrimp marry to create a peppery sweet salad that is certain to please all palates.

Patsy's Chopped Salad

Patsy's, courtesy of Sal Scognamillo

1 small head iceberg lettuce,
   rinsed and coarsely chopped
2 medium ripe, firm tomatoes, chopped
4 anchovy fillets, drained
   from oil, chopped
1/2 cup pimiento peppers, chopped
Salt and freshly ground black
   pepper to taste

DRESSING
1/2 cup extra virgin olive oil
1/4 cup red wine vinegar
1 clove garlic, minced
1 tablespoon chopped fresh Italian parsley
Salt and freshly ground pepper to taste
Pinch of dried oregano

SERVES 4

In a salad bowl, gently toss the lettuce, tomatoes, anchovies, and pimiento peppers.

Sprinkle with salt and pepper.

In a screw-top jar or cruet, combine the dressing ingredients. Cover tightly and shake until thoroughly blended. Gradually spoon dressing over salad and toss to combine.

A traditional salad of crisp and crunchy bite-size pieces, chopped salad is perfect for one-forker buffets or picnics. Anchovies add that special taste but may be served separately to suit each guest.

Ensaladilla Rusa

Sangria 46, courtesy of Benny Castro

6–7 medium white potatoes, unpeeled

1–1 ½ cups mayonnaise

2 roasted red peppers (bottled), 1 coarsely chopped, 1 thinly sliced

1 (6-ounce) can tuna in oil

1 (16-ounce) can peas and carrots, drained

2 hard-boiled eggs, 1 coarsely chopped, 1 thinly sliced

Salt and freshly ground pepper to taste

6 white asparagus (bottled), drained

SERVES 4–6

In a large pot, cook potatoes in salted boiling water until tender, about 20–25 minutes.

When tender, remove and set aside to cool. When potatoes are cool, cut into ½-inch dice and place in a large bowl. Carefully fold in the mayonnaise. Add the chopped peppers, tuna, peas and carrots, and chopped egg and blend well. Season to taste with the salt and pepper. Place the salad in a decorative serving bowl and smooth the top.

Decorate the top in a design of your choice with the pepper strips, sliced egg, and asparagus spears. Serve cold or at room temperature.

Spain's version of Russian potato salad is most often served as a tapa, but it is great as a side salad with assorted meats and cheeses. Always a comfort, this potato salad is sure to please all.

Iridium Salad

Iridium Jazz Club, courtesy of Brian Heyman

1 cup vegetable oil
¼ cup balsamic vinegar
2 shallots, minced
4–6 cups mixed greens

12 cherry tomatoes, halved
⅓ cup toasted pecan pieces
½ cup crumbled bleu cheese

SERVES 4

Place oil, vinegar, and shallots in a food processor, blend well, and chill.

Divide greens and tomatoes among chilled salad plates. Sprinkle with pecan pieces and bleu cheese. Drizzle with 2–3 tablespoons dressing, more or less to taste. Extra dressing will keep in the refrigerator for a week.

A balsamic vinaigrette is one of the most popular salad dressings. While some balsamics are extremely expensive, good-quality ones are available for affordable prices in most supermarkets.

Baby Arugula with Crispy Prosciutto

Algonquin Hotel, courtesy of Alex Aubry

8 slices prosciutto
4–6 cups baby arugula
16 grape tomatoes, halved
1 cup shaved Parmesan cheese

DRESSING
¾ extra virgin olive oil
¼ cup lemon juice
1 tablespoon honey
Salt and pepper to taste

SERVES 4

Preheat oven to 425 degrees F.

Place prosciutto slices on a sheet pan and crisp in the oven until firm, about 8 minutes.

Combine dressing ingredients and shake well. Toss arugula with the dressing and divide among salad plates. Top each with 2 prosciutto slices and 8 tomato halves. Divide Parmesan shavings among the plates and serve.

A simple-to-make salad takes on a more complex taste with the addition of delectable oven-crisped prosciutto. A basic honey and lemon dressing further brings out a burst of flavor.

Frankie & Johnnie's Special

Frankie & Johnnie's Steakhouse, courtesy of Peter Chimos

DRESSING

½ cup extra virgin olive oil
¼ cup red wine vinegar
Salt and pepper to taste

SALAD

4–6 cups coarsely chopped iceberg lettuce
2 medium tomatoes, cut in 1-inch dice
1 roasted red pepper (bottled), chopped
1 cup cucumber, cut in ½-inch dice
½ cup chopped green bell pepper
½ cup thinly sliced white mushrooms
¼ cup chopped red onion
8 anchovy fillets, drained and minced

SERVES 4

Whisk together the oil, vinegar, salt, and pepper. Set aside.

In a large salad bowl, toss all salad ingredients until well mixed. Add ¼ cup vinaigrette and toss. Drizzle in additional vinaigrette according to taste. Serve with freshly ground pepper.

This salad is a vegetable lover's delight with seven garden-fresh veggies. Simply dressed with olive oil and red wine vinegar, it can be a highlight for any occasion.

Waldorf Salad

Market Diner, courtesy of Steve Karakatsanis

4 tablespoons olive oil

1½ tablespoons balsamic vinegar

Salt and pepper to taste

4–6 cups mesclun

1 apple, peeled, cored, and
  cut in ¼-inch slices

½ cup dried cranberries

¼ cup chopped walnuts

SERVES 4

Whisk together the oil, vinegar, salt, and pepper until well combined.

In a decorative salad bowl, toss the mesclun, apple slices, cranberries, and walnuts in the vinaigrette and serve.

Order "a Waldorf" and salad doesn't have to be said. Probably one of the best-known salads, it originated at New York City's Waldorf Astoria in the nineteenth century. Add sliced grilled chicken and it becomes an amazing entrée.

Belgian Endive, Roquefort, and Roasted Walnut Salad

Chez Josephine, courtesy of Frank Diaz

1 cup chopped walnuts
1 teaspoon egg white
¼ teaspoon curry powder
⅛ teaspoon salt
4 large endive

DRESSING
2 tablespoons walnut oil
1 tablespoon plus 1 teaspoon
   extra virgin olive oil
2 teaspoons Chardonnay vinegar
Salt and freshly ground pepper to taste

¼ cup crumbled Roquefort cheese

SERVES 4

Preheat oven to 375-degrees F.

Toss the walnuts, egg white, curry powder, and salt and place on a baking sheet. Roast in oven 10–15 minutes, being careful not to burn.

Do not separate endive leaves but slice each lengthwise into 4 equal slices.

Combine dressing ingredients in a screw-top jar, cover tightly, and shake until well blended.

Fan each sliced endive on salad plates. Drizzle with dressing and sprinkle with roasted walnuts and Roquefort.

Cigar-shaped endive is grown in the dark to avoid its turning green and, because it is a member of the chicory family, it is slightly bitter. A favorite complement to its flavor is Roquefort, also known as the "king of cheeses."

"What's it like working at a New York City landmark hotel in the Theater District? For almost thirty years I've served theater actors, movie stars, journalists, authors, and politicians in a fantastic environment. Can't complain about that! And the people I work with are family. One of our favorite times is on New Year's Eve when all the wait staff dress up in white tablecloths and bang pots and pans to welcome in the New Year. This tradition was there way before my time and I'm sure it will be there long after."

—Gulfer "Chuck" Shah, Algonquin Hotel

Popeye's Spinach Salad

Ellen's Stardust Diner, courtesy of Brian Heyman

1 cup vegetable oil
¼ cup balsamic vinegar
2 shallots, minced
4–6 cups fresh baby spinach

3 large tomatoes, coarsely chopped
4 hard-boiled eggs, quartered
½ cup crumbled bleu cheese

SERVES 4

Place the oil, vinegar, and shallots in a food processor and blend. Place in a nonreactive container and chill in refrigerator.

Divide spinach among salad plates and top with tomatoes, eggs, and bleu cheese. Drizzle 2–3 tablespoons vinaigrette over each salad. Extra vinaigrette will keep in the refrigerator for a week.

{ Baby spinach is ideal for salads because of its tenderness. But don't be fooled, it will make you as strong as Popeye. }

Red and Yellow Beet Salad

Russian Tea Room, courtesy of Marc Taxiera

2 large red beets, cooked and
    peeled, skin reserved
2 large yellow beets, cooked and
    peeled, skins discarded
1 cup ginger juice, divided
¼ cup sherry vinegar

1 cup canola oil
½ cup water
Salt and pepper to taste
4–6 cups baby arugula
1 cup toasted chopped walnuts
½ cup crumbled bleu cheese

SERVES 4

Cut the beets into ¼-inch dice but keep them separated to prevent colors bleeding together. Marinate the beets separately, each in ½ cup ginger juice, for about 1 hour. Place the red beet trimmings, vinegar, oil, and water in a blender and blend until smooth. Season to taste with salt and pepper.

On individual plates, sprinkle the beets in a circle, leaving space in the middle for the arugula. Sprinkle the walnuts over the beets.

Toss the arugula with the vinaigrette and place in the center of each plate. Top the salads with bleu cheese. Serve with crusty rustic bread.

Ginger juice is simply the liquid extracted from gingerroot. While it can be done at home, it is available in health food stores and in specialty markets.

Gorgonzola and Mango Salad

Market Diner, courtesy of Steve Karakatsanis

1 cup fresh orange juice

1 tablespoon sugar

1 teaspoon cornstarch

1 ripe mango, sliced lengthwise
into ¼-inch slices

3 tablespoons olive oil

1 tablespoon balsamic vinegar

Salt and pepper to taste

4–6 cups mixed field greens

3 plum tomatoes, cut in half lengthwise

½ cup chopped walnuts

1 small red onion, thinly sliced

¼–⅓ cup crumbled Gorgonzola cheese

SERVES 4

Mix the orange juice, sugar, and cornstarch until well combined. Add mango slices and refrigerate, stirring occasionally, for 1–2 hours.

Whisk the oil, vinegar, salt, and pepper until combined.

In a large salad bowl, toss the mixed greens with the oil mixture. Add the tomatoes, walnuts, and onion and gently toss. Top with the marinated mango slices and then sprinkle with Gorgonzola cheese and serve.

An easy-to-make salad, this one is taken to greater heights with the topping of mango slices that have been marinated in orange juice and sugar.

This quick and healthy chicken salad is an ideal refreshing spring and summertime meal. Drizzled with a classic French aioli dressing, this salad takes on the perfect Dijonaise zip.

Le Petit
un deux trois
Restaurant Jardin

1-2-3 Chicken Salad

Café Un Deux Trois, courtesy of Luis Gonzalez

GARLIC AIOLI DRESSING
5 cloves garlic, minced
3 egg yolks
1 teaspoon Dijon mustard
1 cup canola oil
Juice from 1/2 lemon

1 pound chicken breasts
3 tablespoons canola oil
Salt and pepper to taste

SALAD
1 (2-pound) package mesclun
1/2 cup sun-dried tomatoes, reconstituted
    and cut into 1/4-inch strips
1/3 cup thinly sliced Bermuda onion
10 fresh basil leaves
1 tablespoon chopped Italian parsley
1/4 cup extra virgin olive oil

SERVES 4

For the dressing, whisk together the garlic, egg yolks, and mustard. In a slow stream, whisk in the oil. (Must be slow to prevent dressing from separating.) Add the lemon juice and blend well. Set aside.

Lightly coat chicken breasts with oil and season with salt and pepper. Grill over medium-high heat for 3 minutes on each side, or until internal temperature reaches 160 degrees.

When cooked, cut the breast into 1/2-inch strips.

Toss all salad ingredients together. Divide salad and chicken on plates and drizzle with the dressing.

"In the 1950s, when I was assistant manager of the Palace Theater, a night's work ended with a midnight show, which consisted of eight acts of vaudeville for 75 minutes and a film lasting 75–90 minutes. After 3 a.m., overtime became an issue, so the curtain had to go down! It's different today, but the excitement of Broadway continues."

—Phil Smith, chairman, Shubert Organization

Avocado Salad with Mango Dressing

Victor's Café, courtesy of Fernando Marulanda

MANGO DRESSING
½ cup mango juice
¼ cup olive oil
2 tablespoons rice vinegar
¼ ripe mango, peeled and chopped
¼ cup chopped scallions
Salt and pepper to taste

SALAD
4 ripe avocados
½ cup coarsely chopped red onion
½ cup watercress

SERVES 4

In a blender, blend the mango juice, oil, vinegar, and mango. Remove, stir in the scallions, salt, and pepper and chill.

Peel, pit, and slice the avocados. Fan out each avocado, pit-side down, on salad plates. Divide onion and watercress on the plates and drizzle with the dressing.

{ The tropical pairing of avocado and mango creates a salad that is not only brilliantly colored but also light and refreshing. }

Caprino Salad

Basso56, courtesy of Paolo Marco Catini

3 tablespoons olive oil
1 tablespoon balsamic vinegar
Salt and pepper to taste
4–6 cups organic baby arugula

1 D'Anjou pear
4 tablespoons goat cheese
Pink peppercorns

SERVES 4

In a large mixing bowl, thoroughly whisk the oil, vinegar, salt, and pepper until the dressing thickens slightly. Toss the dressing with the baby arugula.

Core and slice the pear lengthwise into ⅛-inch slices. (A mandoline is useful here.)

On each salad plate, layer one-fourth of the pear slices in a clockwise pattern. Divide the salad in the center of the plates. Top each with 1 tablespoon goat cheese. Sprinkle with pink peppercorns.

A salad of arugula, pear, and cheese is sprinkled with slightly sweet pink peppercorns. Don't let the name deceive you, as they are not actually peppercorns but rather dried berries from a rose plant.

Salad of Mission Figs, Baby Fennel, Frisee, Pecorino, and Italian Truffle

**Lucille's Grill at B.B. King,
courtesy of Master Chef Erik Blauberg**

DRESSING

¼ cup fresh lime juice
½ teaspoon Dijon mustard
3 tablespoons truffle oil or grape seed oil
¼ cup olive oil

SALAD

8 black mission figs, cut in half lengthwise
8 bulbs baby fennel, peeled and shaved
1 head green endive, separated
1 head red endive, separated
2 heads frisee (centers only),
    cut in 2-inch lengths
½ cup shaved Pecorino Toscano
1 black truffle (golf-ball size), diced small
Fleur de sel to taste
Freshly ground white pepper to taste

SERVES 4

For the dressing, whisk the lime juice and mustard in a stainless steel bowl. Combine the oils and gradually whisk into the lime juice and mustard.

On large, decorative salad plates, divide the salad ingredients, creating your own design.

Drizzle with the dressing and sprinkle with the salt and pepper.

For that special dinner party, this is the "king of salads" with its black truffle And let's not forget to thank the Franciscan missionaries who first brought luscious black figs from Spain to Southern California, thus mission figs.

soups

Gazpacho with Shrimp

Sardi's, courtesy of Patrick Piñon

1 slice crustless white bread,
  cut into 1-inch cubes

2 tablespoons sherry vinegar, divided

¼ cup water

2 pounds very ripe tomatoes

2 cloves garlic, minced

½ cup finely diced cucumber

½ cup finely diced onion

½ cup finely diced red bell pepper

3 tablespoons olive oil

Salt and pepper to taste

3 tablespoons finely diced
  cucumber to garnish

3 tablespoons finely diced red
  bell pepper to garnish

6 large cooked shrimp, halved

SERVES 6

In a large bowl, soak the bread cubes in 1 tablespoon vinegar and water. Dip tomatoes in a stockpot of boiling salted water for about 30–45 seconds. Transfer to a bowl of ice water to loosen the skin. Remove skins, dice coarsely, and add to bowl with the bread. Stir in garlic, cucumber, onion, bell pepper, oil, and the remaining vinegar. Place all ingredients in a blender and puree until smooth. Season to taste with salt and pepper. Refrigerate until well chilled. To serve, ladle soup among soup bowls and garnish with cucumber and bell pepper. Top each with 2 shrimp halves and serve.

Thoughts of southern Spain bring to mind sun and the smell of the Mediterranean. This famous cold, uncooked soup from the Andalusian region captures that feeling and taste. Sun-drenched vegetables and shrimp bring the land and the sea together in this summertime favorite.

Pasta e Fagioli

La Rivista, courtesy of Luciano Marchignoli

¼ cup olive oil

3 cloves garlic, minced

1 (2-ounce) chunk pancetta

¼ cup finely chopped parsley

4 cups water

2 tablespoons tomato paste

1 (19-ounce) can cannellini
  beans, drained and rinsed

1 ½ cups ditalini pasta

Salt and pepper to taste

⅓ cup freshly grated Parmesan cheese

SERVES 4

In a large stockpot, heat the oil over medium-high heat. Add the garlic, pancetta, and parsley and sauté until lightly brown. Stir in water, tomato paste, and beans and bring to a boil. Reduce heat to medium-low, add ditalini, salt, and pepper and simmer 30–35 minutes. Add more water if needed. Ladle into soup bowls, drizzle with oil, and sprinkle with Parmesan cheese. Serve with crusty Italian bread.

This hearty Italian "pasta and beans" soup uses ditalini, "little thimbles," and cannellini, Italian white kidney beans. Flavored with pancetta, this classic is a meal in itself.

"It was an audition for Bob Fosse's *Dancin'*. Hundreds of dancers auditioning—a cattle call. I went through a number of eliminations and finally was on the stage by myself. Mr. Fosse came up on the stage, bent down on one knee, resting his elbow on the other, and stared straight ahead at my legs. Then I was told to do the routine we'd been taught. Mr. Fosse continued to stare at my legs, never lifting his eyes above knee level, never uttering a word. I was so unnerved that I messed up some of the steps. Needless to say, I didn't get the job. Perhaps it was for the better. Stories ran rampant in the dance community after the show opened that it was such a killer to do and the dancers had so many injuries that they needed to be continually on pain killers."

—Diane Boardman, dancer/choreographer

French Onion Soup

Maison, courtesy of Mario Urgiles

3 tablespoons olive oil
3 tablespoons unsalted butter
4 medium onions, sliced
2 cloves garlic, minced
2 sprigs fresh lemon thyme
   or a pinch of dried
½ cup dry red wine

¼ cup sherry vinegar
¼ cup just-melted sugar
4 cups veal stock
Salt and pepper to taste
6 toasted brioche slices
2–3 cups grated Gruyère cheese

SERVES 6

In a large, heavy stockpot, heat oil and butter over medium heat. Add onions and cook until soft and golden brown. Stir in the garlic and thyme and cook until flavors blend, about 3–4 minutes. Stir in the wine, vinegar, and melted sugar and cook for 5 minutes. Add the stock, bring to a boil, and season with salt and pepper. Lower heat and simmer 2–3 hours.

In six ovenproof bowls, place a slice of brioche, ladle soup over top and sprinkle with cheese. Place under the broiler until the cheese melts and begins to brown. Serve immediately.

The key to this centuries-old French classic is the caramelizing of the onions and rich veal stock. Here buttery toasted brioche placed on the bottom of each bowl adds a delightful change from the traditional French baguette.

Sopa de Ajo

Meson Sevilla, courtesy of Joaquin Lucero

6 cups chicken stock
1/3 cup extra virgin olive oil
6–8 large cloves garlic,
   crushed and chopped
6 slices white bread, cubed

1 teaspoon paprika
Salt to taste
4 eggs
Chopped parsley to garnish

SERVES 4

In a large stockpot, bring the stock to a boil.

In a large, heavy skillet, heat the oil over medium heat. Add garlic and sauté until light brown. Add bread cubes, paprika, and salt and cook until bread cubes are golden brown. Add the skillet ingredients to the chicken stock. Bring to a boil, reduce heat and simmer 8–10 minutes. Remove pot from stove and then gradually beat in the eggs. Garnish with parsley and serve piping hot.

This popular soup of Spain is a celebration of that glorious little bulb, garlic. Typically a peasant dish, this soup is fortified with bread and eggs to create an inexpensive, simple yet delicious comfort food.

If you love cold, creamy vichyssoise in the summer, then you will love this winter version. Same ingredients but with "comfort" chunks of potato and leek and served hot.

Chunky Potato Leek Soup

Café Un Deux Trois, courtesy of Luis Gonzalez

12 medium leeks

1 stick unsalted butter

2 ½ pounds russet potatoes,
   cut into 2-inch chunks

3 cups chicken or vegetable stock

3 fresh thyme sprigs

3 bay leaves

Salt and pepper to taste

SERVES 8

Cut leeks into 1-inch pieces and soak in water two to three times (changing water each time) to remove all dirt. Drain thoroughly.

In a large stockpot, melt the butter over low heat. Add leeks and sauté, stirring often, until tender but not browned, about 20 minutes. Stir in potatoes, stock, thyme, bay leaves, salt, and pepper and bring to a boil. Reduce heat and simmer until the potatoes are tender and flavors blend, about 30–40 minutes. Remove thyme sprigs and bay leaves and serve hot with warm, crusty bread.

Boeuf Bourguignon

Café Un Deux Trois, courtesy of Luis Gonzalez

4 pounds beef shoulder, cut
  into 1½-inch cubes
2 stalks celery, cut into 2-inch pieces
2 carrots, cut into 2-inch pieces
2 large onions, quartered

4 cloves garlic, halved
12 juniper berries
4 liters red wine (preferably
  Pinot Noir or Beaujolais)
Juice of 2 oranges

SERVES 6

In a large, heavy stockpot, combine all ingredients except oil, flour, bacon, mushrooms, and pearl onions. Marinate in the refrigerator for 24 hours to allow meat to absorb all the flavors.

Strain the meat and vegetables, reserving the liquid.

In the same stockpot, heat a few tablespoons oil over medium-high heat. Dredge the meat cubes in flour (adding a little oil as needed) and brown in batches in the hot oil until golden brown on all sides. Set aside the meat on a platter. Add the vegetables to the stockpot and sauté 3–4 minutes. Return meat and

Cooked "in the style of Burgundy," this slow-simmered classic French beef stew blends the typical ingredients of red wine, bacon, mushrooms, and pearl onions to create the ultimate comfort food.

2 sprigs each fresh thyme and rosemary
2 bay leaves
Canola oil for browning and sautéing
Flour for dredging

¼ pound bacon, chopped,
    cooked crisp, and drained
1 pound white mushrooms
1 pound pearl onions

reserved liquid to the pot and bring to a boil. Reduce heat and simmer over medium-low for 2 hours, or until meat is tender.

Strain and discard the vegetables. Return the liquid to the fire and boil to reduce by half.

While reducing, sauté mushrooms and pearl onions in oil over medium heat until light brown. Add the meat, bacon, mushrooms and onions to the pot and simmer for 5–6 minutes. Serve with boiled potatoes.

Bean and Tubetti Soup

Patsy's, courtesy of Sal Scognamillo

2 cups uncooked tubetti pasta
¼ cup olive oil
1 cup chopped onion
2 cups chicken or vegetable stock

1 (15-ounce) can cannellini
    beans, drained and rinsed
3 cups Patsy's Marinara Sauce
Salt and freshly ground pepper to taste

SERVES 6

Cook pasta according to package directions.

In a large, heavy soup pot, heat the oil over medium-high heat. Sauté onion until lightly brown, about 3–4 minutes. Add the stock, beans, and marinara sauce and bring to a boil. Stir in the drained, cooked pasta, reduce heat and simmer 3–4 minutes. Season with salt and pepper. Serve piping hot with warm Italian bread.

Tubetti —"little tubes"—are used in this popular Italian bean and pasta soup frequently served at weddings. If tubetti is not readily available, macaroni can be substituted.

"Part of the excitement of the Theater District is a one-time annual event when millions gather to ring in the New Year. I've been lucky enough to be a part of that celebration for over thirty-five years. Strangely enough, this event is put together by a handful of devoted people, who separate themselves from the festivities and work hard to pull off the world's biggest party. This Times Square extravaganza is a part of what makes the entire Theater District the place to be on New Year's Eve."

—Dick Clark, host, *Dick Clark's New Year's Rockin' Eve*

Senegalese Soup

'21' Club, courtesy of John Greeley

2 tablespoons butter
2 cups ½-inch dice onions
2 cups ½-inch dice leeks, white part only
2 cups ½-inch dice Granny Smith apples
2 tablespoons flour
¼ cup Madras curry powder
3 cups chicken stock
½ cup heavy cream
Salt to taste

GARNISHES

2 cups cooked and cooled ½-inch diced chicken breast
½ cup ¼-inch dice Granny Smith apple
2 tablespoons chopped celery leaves
2 tablespoons fresh chopped chives
1 teaspoon curry powder

SERVES 4

In a large soup pot, melt the butter over medium heat. Add onions, leeks, and apples and cook, stirring occasionally, until transparent, about 10 minutes. Blend in flour and cook over medium heat an additional 3–4 minutes. Do not brown. Stir in curry powder and stock. Reduce heat to low and simmer 15–20 minutes. Remove from heat and set aside to cool. When completely cooled, puree in a blender until smooth. Blend in the cream, season with salt, and chill until ready to serve.

To serve, ladle soup into chilled bowls and garnish with the chicken, apple, celery, chives, and curry powder.

This rich curried apple soup uses basic ingredients and simple preparation to create complex flavors. A special touch is the diced chicken breast used as a garnish rather than an ingredient. Chilling heightens the taste and is ideal for summer.

Zuppa di Broccoli

Lattanzi, courtesy of Carla Lattanzi

3 tablespoons olive oil
3 cloves garlic, minced
2 cups broccoli florets
5 cups fish or vegetable stock

2 tablespoons tomato sauce
1 cup broken angel hair pasta
Salt and red pepper to taste

SERVES 4

In a large, heavy stockpot, heat the oil over medium-high heat. Add the garlic and sauté until lightly browned, about 2–3 minutes. Add the broccoli and sauté until the oil is absorbed. Stir in the stock and tomato sauce and bring to a slow boil. Cook until broccoli is tender, about 4–5 minutes. Add the pasta and cook until pasta is al dente, about 2–3 minutes. Season to taste with salt and red pepper.

{ Broccoli, a relative of the cabbage, is available year-round, making this a quick, delicious and healthy soup for any day. }

Russian Borscht

Russian Tea Room, courtesy of Marc Taxiera

1 tablespoon olive oil

8 ounces smoked bacon, without the fat

1½ cups shredded cabbage

½ cup chopped onion

½ cup chopped carrots

½ cup chopped celery

½ cup mashed potatoes

3½ cups chicken stock

1 pound roasted beets, half julienned and the other half diced, liquid reserved

2 tablespoons red wine vinegar

Salt and pepper to taste

2 tablespoons chopped fresh dill

Sour cream and fresh dill sprigs to garnish

SERVES 4

In a large, heavy stockpot, heat the oil over medium-high heat. Cook bacon until lightly browned, about 3–4 minutes. Fold in cabbage, onion, carrots, and celery and cook until transparent, about 6–8 minutes. Stir in the mashed potatoes, stock, reserved beet liquid, vinegar, salt, and pepper. Lower heat to medium and simmer soup, stirring occasionally, about 10–12 minutes. Add the beets and continue to cook 5 minutes. Stir in the dill. Ladle hot soup into individual soup bowls, dollop with sour cream and garnish with dill sprigs. Serve with thick slices of black bread and lots of butter.

When Russia and soup are used in the same sentence, borscht immediately comes to mind. This traditional Russian dish can be served hot or cold. Here is the hot version for those frigid, snowy nights.

Traditional Chicken Noodle Soup

Frankie & Johnnie's Steakhouse, courtesy of Peter Chimos

2 tablespoons olive oil
3 cloves garlic, minced
½ cup diced celery
½ cup diced carrots
10 cups chicken stock

3 cups cooked ½-inch dice chicken breast
8 ounces wide egg noodles
Salt and pepper to taste
¼ cup fresh chopped parsley

SERVES 6–8

In a large, heavy stockpot, heat oil over medium-high heat. Add the garlic, celery, and carrots and sauté 4–5 minutes. Add the stock and chicken, reduce heat and simmer 10–12 minutes. Add the noodles and simmer 10–15 minutes, or until tender. Season to taste with salt and pepper. Sprinkle with parsley.

Probably one of the most popular soups loved by all ages is so simple to make and so much more delicious than canned. Double up, freeze, and have a handy meal on short notice.

Garden Vegetable Soup

Ellen's Stardust Diner, courtesy of Brian Heyman

3 tablespoons olive oil
2 cups fresh spinach
1 cup diced white mushrooms
1/2 cup diced celery
1/2 cup diced carrots

1/2 cup chopped tomatoes
6 cups chicken or vegetable stock
1/4 cup tomato puree
Salt and pepper to taste

SERVES 4–6

In a large, heavy stockpot, heat the oil over medium-high heat. Add all vegetables and sauté 4–5 minutes. Add the stock and bring to a boil. Stir in the tomato puree, reduce heat to medium, and simmer 30–40 minutes. Season to taste with salt and pepper.

{ Five vegetables from your garden or farmers market simmered in stock makes a fresh and light soup that will delight everyone. }

pasta

Stracci translates literally to "scraps." It's the pasta dough that remains after the shaped pasta is made. In place of homemade stracci, you can use uncooked lasagna strips, broken up.

Stracci Alle Fave

Trattoria Dopo Teatro, courtesy of Roberto Lamorte

PASTA

1 pound flour

4 eggs

1/2 cup olive oil

1/2 teaspoon salt

FAVA BEANS

1 cup frozen fava beans

2 tablespoons olive oil

1 clove garlic, chopped

2 slices pancetta or bacon, cubed

1/2 tablespoon chopped rosemary

1/2 tablespoon chopped fresh sage

1/2 tablespoon chopped fresh thyme

1 cup white wine

Salt and pepper to taste

1/2 cup shaved Parmesan cheese

SERVES 4

To make the pasta, mix all ingredients well to form a soft dough. Roll out with a floured rolling pin and tear into pieces, or "scraps." Set aside on wax paper and allow to dry until ready to use.

In a large pot of boiling water, cook the fava beans for 2 minutes. Remove the fava beans, reserve the water, and keep at a boil. Cool the fava beans and when cooled, peel and set aside.

In a large, heavy skillet, heat the oil over medium heat. Add the garlic and sauté about 2 minutes. Add the pancetta or bacon and cook until crispy. Add the rosemary, sage, thyme, wine, salt, and pepper. Cook until wine reduces to 1/2 cup, then add 1 cup of the fava bean water. Add the fava beans and simmer for 2 minutes. Set aside and keep warm while pasta cooks.

For the homemade pasta, add to boiling fava bean water and cook about 4–5 minutes. If using store-bought pasta, cook according to package directions. Drain the pasta, fold into skillet with sauce and blend well. Divide among pasta bowls or plates and top with shaved Parmesan cheese.

Linguine Alle Vongole

Orso, courtesy of Victor Flores

½ cup extra virgin olive oil
6 cloves garlic, thinly sliced
½ cup chopped flat-leaf Italian parsley
1 tablespoon red pepper flakes
1 cup dry white wine

40 cockle clams, scrubbed
1 pound fresh minced clams
1½ cups canned clam juice
1 pound dried linguine
Salt and pepper to taste

SERVES 4

In a large, heavy pot, heat the oil over medium-high heat. Add the garlic and sauté until golden brown. Stir in the parsley and red pepper flakes. Add the wine, raise the heat, and bring to a boil. Add the cockle clams, minced clams, and clam juice. Cover and cook until clams open, about 3–4 minutes.

Cook the pasta according to package directions and drain well. Fold the pasta into the pot of clams and cook over high heat for 2 minutes. Season with salt and pepper and serve immediately.

Pasta and small saltwater cockle clams come together and give more meaning to the old expression "warms the cockles of my heart." Quick and easy, this dish is sure to provide comfort and contentment.

Garganelli with Prosciutto and Spring Peas

La Rivista, courtesy of Luciano Marchignoli

1 (16-ounce) box garganelli
2 tablespoons olive oil
8 ounces proscuitto, small diced
1 cup frozen peas, thawed

½ cup dry white wine
2 cups heavy cream
½ cup grated Parmesan cheese
Freshly grated black pepper to taste

SERVES 4

Cook the pasta according to package directions. While pasta is cooking, make the sauce.

In a large, heavy skillet, heat the oil over medium heat. Add the proscuitto and sauté until crispy. Stir in the peas and wine and reduce for about 2–3 minutes. Stir in the cream, cheese, and pepper and bring just to a boil. Reduce heat to very low and stir frequently while pasta finishes cooking.

Drain pasta and blend into the sauce skillet. Serve with additional Parmesan cheese and black pepper, if desired.

Garganelli is an egg pasta that is shaped like a small, ridged tube. If garganelli is not readily available, penne rigate is the perfect substitute.

"Auditioning for Broadway is great. How else can you get to sing on the stage of a landmark Broadway theater and personally meet some of the most famous directors and producers? Even if you don't get the job, you leave the theater saying, 'Wow, guess who I just met!'

"Auditioning can be exiting. I was standing in an audition line and at Radio City Music Hall with 800 other people. I finally got in to sing, and immediately after, the director gave me a nod and a wink; I suddenly felt so high. Did that mean he liked my singing? After not leaving my phone for two days, the call came in. I got the job!"

—Lucy Jarvis, Executive Producer

The New York Times

A Fiery New Incarnation of a Monster of a Mother

By CHARLES ISHERWOOD

July 16, 2008

It's really not a good idea to mess with Violet Weston, the fire-breathing dragon lady of Pawhuska, Okla., who presides over a feast of family combat in "August: Osage County." As all who have seen Tracy Letts's celebrated comedy-drama on Broadway no doubt vividly recall, Violet does not brook much interference when it comes to indulging her favorite pastimes.

Raise an objection to that eviscerating commentary on her daughter's looks and you are liable to be mercilessly dissected. Delicately suggest that airing the family's dirtiest laundry might be subjected to eyebrow-singeing.

Oh, and don't even think about messing with the little bottles of pills that are never far from her grasp. That would be a sure way to lose a limb.

Violet is a maternal monster for the ages, but she is also one of the most vivid and memorable characters to stalk a Broadway stage in recent years. Estelle Parsons, the new star cast in this demanding role, does not disappoint her much.

All the hallmarks of the character — the crackling cruelty, the shrill self-pity, the unbending will of iron — are present and accounted for in her superb performance.

She is a naturalistic actress, and her interpretation is as incongruously warm as it is appalling. When she sees that she has drawn blood, yet she almost relishes the very wounds that she herself inflicts.

act, when Violet of terror, Ms. affectionate when she reveals a grim portrait feeling in her Ms. Parsons (Bonnie and Clyde) a director seen on Broadway of which but much in recent years her past was at Seven and also

drug-fueled reign of the casually fearful shrew. But that provides

Robert Foxworth resignation as Mayor rebellion against audience-rousing comfortably in the philandering

Calamarata Mare and Monti

Bistecca Fiorentina, courtesy of Luciano Marchignoli

1 pound calamarata
¼ cup olive oil
4 cloves garlic, minced
1 teaspoon red pepper flakes
1 cup coarsely chopped white mushrooms
2 cups white wine

1 cup lobster meat
2 tablespoons unsalted butter
2 tablespoons tomato paste
Coarsely chopped Italian
  parsley to garnish

SERVES 4

Cook pasta according to package directions; reserving ¼ cup pasta water when done.

In a large, heavy skillet, heat the oil over medium heat. Add garlic and sauté until brown. Add the pepper flakes, mushrooms and wine and cook for 5 minutes. Blend in the lobster, butter and tomato paste with ¼ cup pasta water. Toss the drained pasta with the sauce and serve immediately. Sprinkle with the parsley.

Calamarata is a wide, tubular, ring-shaped pasta. It's ideal for this Italian version of surf 'n' turf using lobster from the sea and mushrooms from the earth.

Rigatoni Sorrentino

Patsy's, courtesy of Sal Scognamillo

1 (16-ounce) box rigatoni
4 cups Patsy's Marinara Sauce
8 ounces fresh ricotta cheese
2 cups grated mozzarella

1½ cups freshly grated
   Parmigiano-Reggiano
Salt and pepper to taste

SERVES 4–6

Cook the pasta according to package directions.

In a large, heavy saucepan, heat the marinara sauce over medium-high heat to the boiling point. Remove from heat and pour half the sauce into a bowl. Return the saucepan to the heat and fold in the ricotta and drained pasta until thoroughly combined. Pour the mixture into a 9 x 13-inch baking dish that has been lightly greased with olive oil, and cover with the reserved sauce. Sprinkle the mozzarella and Parmigiano-Reggiano over top. Place under the broiler until the cheeses melt, about 6–8 minutes.

Serve piping hot with a cold, crisp salad and a loaf of country bread.

This easy-to-make, three-cheese casserole with large-grooved pasta is the perfect family meal or casual get-together buffet dish.

Duck confit, also known as "confit de canard," is a product of a centuries-old process of salt-curing and poaching in duck fat. Luckily, confit is available in cans and can be refrigerated for months.

Spinach Tagliatelle with Duck Confit and Exotic Mushrooms

Algonquin Hotel, courtesy of Alex Aubry

1 pound spinach tagliatelle
½ cup olive oil, divided
2 cloves garlic, minced
1 cup fresh exotic mushrooms,
  such as oyster, horn of plenty,
  lobster, baby shiitake

1 cup frozen peas, thawed
1½ cups duck confit
½ cup heavy cream
Salt and pepper to taste
Freshly grated Parmesan
  cheese to garnish

SERVES 4

Cook pasta according to package directions.

In a large, heavy skillet, heat ¼ cup oil over medium-high heat. Add garlic and mushrooms and sauté 3–4 minutes. Blend in the peas, confit, and cream and cook an additional 2–3 minutes until heated through. Toss with the drained pasta and blend in the remaining oil. Plate and serve with Parmesan cheese and crusty French bread.

Tagliolini Verdi Gamberetti e Zucchine

Lattanzi, courtesy of Carla Lattanzi

½ pound green tagliolini
3 tablespoons olive oil
2 cloves garlic, minced
6 small zucchini, very thinly sliced
1 cup fish stock

¼ cup brandy
¼ cup tomato sauce
1 pound small (36–45 count)
  shrimp, peeled
Salt and red pepper to taste

SERVES 4

Cook pasta according to package directions.

In a large, heavy skillet, heat the oil over medium-high heat and sauté garlic for 2–3 minutes. Add zucchini strips and sauté for 4–5 minutes, stirring constantly. Stir in the stock, brandy, and tomato sauce and simmer 2–3 minutes. Add the shrimp to the sauce and cook until shrimp are opaque, about 2–3 minutes. When pasta is al dente, add to the skillet, gently toss with the sauce and simmer 1–2 minutes. Season to taste with salt and red pepper. Serve family style on a large decorative platter.

Also known as tagliarini, this long, paper-thin pasta is tossed with long strips of zucchini and sweet shrimp. Added richness comes from a brandy-enhanced sauce.

Rigatoni Caprese

Market Diner, courtesy of Steve Karakatsanis

1 pound rigatoni

3 tablespoons olive oil

1 large tomato, coarsely chopped

2–3 cups fresh spinach

Salt and pepper to taste

½ pound grated mozzarella

SERVES 4–6

Preheat oven to 350 degrees.

Cook pasta according to package directions.

In a large, heavy skillet, heat the oil over medium-high heat. Add tomato and spinach and sauté until spinach wilts, about 3–5 minutes. When pasta is cooked, drain and add to skillet. Blend thoroughly with the tomato and spinach, about 30 seconds. Season to taste with salt and pepper. Place in a baking dish, sprinkle with mozzarella and bake until the cheese melts, about 10–12 minutes.

Cooked in the style of the Isle of Capri in Italy, where cooks incorporate tomatoes, mozzarella and basil, this dish has a twist. Basil is replaced with fresh spinach.

Penne Sauce Pistou et Saumon

Café Un Deux Trois, courtesy of Luis Gonzalez

PESTO SAUCE
2 cups fresh basil, well packed
¾ cup olive oil
3 cloves garlic, chopped
1 tablespoon grated Parmesan cheese
Salt and pepper to taste

1 pound penne pasta
4 tablespoons unsalted butter
1 pound fresh Atlantic salmon,
    cut into 1-inch cubes
2 cups heavy cream
½ pound fresh tomatoes, chopped
Salt and pepper to taste
½ cup Pesto Sauce (above)
¼ cup grated Parmesan cheese

SERVES 4

In a food processor, puree all pesto ingredients and set aside.

Cook pasta according to package instructions.

While pasta is cooking, melt butter over medium heat in a large, heavy skillet. Add salmon and sauté over medium-high heat until golden brown, about 1–2 minutes on all sides. Stir in the cream and bring to a boil for 2 minutes. Toss in the tomatoes, salt, and pepper and cook until tomatoes are heated through, about 3–4 minutes. Stir in ½ cup pesto at the last minute to maintain its brilliant green color. Add drained pasta and Parmesan cheese to the skillet and toss well.

Adjust seasonings and serve immediately with a crisp green salad and crusty bread.

Pistou is the French version of the Italian pesto, with its puree of basil, oil, and garlic. This sauce freezes well and can be used in a variety of dishes.

Spaghetti Bolognese

Chez Josephine, courtesy of Frank Diaz

3 tablespoons olive oil
2 cloves garlic, minced
1 cup chopped onion
1/3 cup chopped white mushrooms
1/2 pound ground beef
1 (16-ounce) jar tomato puree
1 cup dry white wine

1 teaspoon tomato paste
2 bay leaves
Salt and pepper to taste
1/2 pound spaghetti
Olive oil
Freshly grated Parmesan cheese

SERVES 4

In a large, heavy skillet, heat the oil over medium-high heat. Add garlic and onion and sauté 4–6 minutes. Stir in the mushrooms and sauté 2 minutes. Add the ground beef and cook until browned and excess moisture has evaporated. Stir in the tomato puree, wine, tomato paste, and bay leaves. Season with salt and pepper and simmer over medium-low heat for 20–30 minutes.

While the sauce simmers, cook pasta according to package directions. When pasta is done, drain and toss it lightly with oil. Place in a large decorative pasta bowl, top with the Bolognese sauce and sprinkle with the Parmesan cheese.

After every performance, this was Josephine Baker's favorite indulgence. While some Bolognese sauces take hours of cooking time, this one takes only a fraction of the time, yet none of the flavor is diminished.

Fettuccine in a Mushroom Cream Sauce

Basso56, courtesy of Paolo Marco Catini

5 ounces dried porcini mushrooms
2 portobello mushroom caps,
    cut in ½-inch slices
10 white champignon mushrooms,
    cut in ½-inch slices
1 tablespoon truffle oil
1 tablespoon fresh chopped rosemary
Salt and pepper to taste

1 tablespoon olive oil
3 cloves garlic, minced
4 cups heavy cream
1 pound fettuccine
Freshly grated Parmesan cheese

SERVES 4

In a bowl, soak the dried porcini mushrooms in 5 cups water for 15–20 minutes. Drain and reserve 1 cup mushroom stock.

Combine all mushrooms, truffle oil, and rosemary and season with salt and pepper.

In a large, heavy skillet, heat olive oil over medium-high heat. Add garlic and sauté 2–3 minutes. Stir in mushrooms and sauté 2–3 minutes. Add 1 cup mushroom stock, bring to a boil, reduce heat to low, and reduce for 3–4 minutes. Add the cream and simmer over low heat until it thickens, about 5–6 minutes. Cook pasta according to package directions. Drain well and fold into the cream sauce. Sprinkle with Parmesan cheese.

Three kinds of mushrooms sautéed with truffle oil and simmered in heavy cream and mushroom stock takes this pasta dish to heavenly heights.

poultry

Marinated Oven-Roasted Chicken with White Wine, Butter, and Lemon Sauce

Orso, courtesy of Victor Flores

MARINADE

1 cup finely chopped fresh rosemary

¾ cup fresh lemon juice

6 cloves garlic, minced

Salt and pepper to taste

2 organic chickens, halved with skin
   and deboned (ask butcher to debone
   them, leaving wing bone intact)

1–2 tablespoons canola oil

WHITE WINE, BUTTER,
   AND LEMON SAUCE

1 tablespoon canola oil

2 shallots, minced

1 cup dry white wine

½ cup chicken stock

½ cup freshly squeezed lemon juice

2 tablespoons unsalted butter

Salt and pepper to taste

SERVES 4

Mix together all ingredients for the marinade. Place chicken in a nonreactive bowl, pour marinade over it and cover with plastic wrap. Marinate in refrigerator overnight.

About 15 minutes before cooking, preheat oven to 500 degrees. Heat a large, heavy skillet over high heat until it begins to smoke. Carefully add canola oil and immediately sear the chicken halves, skin side down, one at a time for about 4–5 minutes. Do not move the chicken while searing to ensure a nice golden and crisp skin. Place chicken on a large baking sheet and bake skin side up for 10–15 minutes.

While chicken bakes, heat 1 tablespoon canola oil over medium heat in the same skillet where chicken was seared. Sauté the shallots until transparent. Add the wine and reduce over high heat until almost evaporated. Add the stock and lemon juice, reduce about 1–2 minutes, and set aside. When ready to serve, bring sauce to a boil, add the butter and whisk vigorously until sauce emulsifies. Pour sauce over chicken and serve immediately.

A simple, classic roasted chicken is a welcome meal anytime. Add a light wine, butter, and lemon sauce and the dish takes on heightened flavor— perfect for a family meal or a dinner party.

Crispy Duck a l'Orange

Café Un Deux Trois, courtesy of Luis Gonzalez

2 (3½-pound) ducks
¼ cup kosher salt

ORANGE SAUCE
2 cups roasted onions

2 cups roasted carrots
2 cups sherry
2 quarts orange juice
1 cinnamon stick
¼ cup red wine vinegar

SERVES 4

Preheat oven to 300 degrees.

Remove large pieces of fat from the ducks. Rub the skin and cavity with the kosher salt. Prick each duck twenty to thirty times and place breast side down in a roasting pan. Roast the ducks slowly for 2 hours to ensure moist meat and crisp skin. Prick the skin every 30 minutes. Drain the fat from the roasting pan and turn the ducks breast side up. Increase oven temperature to 350 degrees and roast ducks an additional 45 minutes, or until skin is crisp. Remove the ducks to a platter, let sit for 10 minutes, and then remove and reserve the backbones.

To make the sauce, heat a large, heavy saucepan. Add all sauce ingredients and the duck backbones. Bring to a boil and continue to boil for 1 hour. Reduce heat if too much evaporation occurs. Return sauce to saucepan and cook over medium heat until sauce becomes a glaze, about 5–10 minutes. While sauce is simmering and becoming a glaze, return the ducks to the oven for 7–10 minutes. Place half of each duck on a plate, nap with orange glaze, and serve with mashed potatoes and a green vegetable.

One of France's best-loved dishes is moist duck with a crunchy skin. Served with a sherry, orange juice, and cinnamon sauce, it is the perfect autumn dinner.

This stuffed, breaded and fried chicken breast dish might not be from the Ukraine, as most have believed. The origin may actually have been New York City in the 1920s. Regardless of its birthplace, it remains an international favorite.

Chicken Kiev

Russian Tea Room, courtesy of Marc Taxiera

1 stick unsalted butter, room temperature
1 teaspoon chopped fresh parsley
1 teaspoon chopped fresh tarragon
1 teaspoon chopped fresh chervil
1 teaspoon chopped fresh dill
Zest from 1 lemon and 1 lime
1 teaspoon kosher salt
¼ teaspoon freshly ground black pepper

4 (4–6-ounce) boneless,
    skinless chicken breasts
Salt and pepper to taste
2 large eggs, slightly beaten
    with 1 teaspoon water
2 cups panko breadcrumbs,
    crushed with a rolling pin
Canola oil for frying

SERVES 4

With a hand mixer, thoroughly blend the butter, herbs, zests, salt, and pepper. Place on plastic wrap or waxed paper, roll into a small log, and place in freezer for 2–3 hours.

Place chicken breasts between two pieces of waxed paper and lightly sprinkle both the chicken and paper with water. Pound the chicken to ⅛-inch thickness.

Lay a chicken breast on a fresh piece of waxed paper and place ¼ of the compound butter in the center. Using the waxed paper to assist, fold in the sides of the breasts and roll tightly into a log, completely enclosing the butter. Continue with the remaining breasts. Place the chicken in the refrigerator for 2–12 hours. When ready to cook, place the egg-and-water mixture in a pie pan and the panko in another. Dip and thoroughly coat the breasts in the egg and then roll in the breadcrumbs.

Place in the refrigerator for 1 hour.

In a large, heavy pot, heat 2 inches oil over medium-high heat until temperature reaches 325 degrees. Gently place breasts in the hot oil and cook until golden brown, about 5–6 minutes on each side. Remove and place on a cooling rack and allow to drain 5–10 minutes before serving.

Pollo Manigua

Victor's Café, courtesy of Fernando Marulanda

MARINADE

½ cup canola oil

2 cloves garlic, chopped

1 tablespoon dried oregano

2 teaspoons salt

1 teaspoon white pepper

4 (4–6-ounce) boneless,
   skinless chicken breasts

2 tablespoons canola oil

SALSA DE MANIGUA

½ cup mango juice

¼ cup white vinegar

¼ cup olive oil

1 scallion, cut in thin strips

1 mango, medium dice

1 avocado, medium dice

Salt to taste

Fresh watercress to garnish

SERVES 4

In a nonreactive bowl, blend marinade ingredients and then add chicken, coating well. Marinate overnight in the refrigerator.

For the salsa, blend the mango juice, vinegar, oil, and scallion. Fold in mango and avocado, taking care not to break the dices. Season to taste with salt and set aside until ready to use.

In a large, heavy skillet, heat 2 tablespoons canola oil over medium-high heat. Remove chicken from marinade and sauté until cooked through and golden brown, about 4–5 minutes on each side, or until the internal temperature reaches 160 degrees. To serve, place chicken breasts on a dinner plate, spoon salsa over top, and garnish with watercress.

A winter night can turn tropical when sautéed chicken breasts are embellished with a deliciously refreshing mango and avocado salsa.

Pollo Extremena

Meson Sevilla, courtesy of Joaquin Lucero

3 cups extra virgin olive oil

3 cloves garlic, coarsely chopped

4 (6–8-ounce) chicken breasts

Flour for dredging

1 large green pepper, cut in ¼-inch strips

1 large onion, cut in ¼-inch strips

2 chorizo sausages, cut in ¼-inch slices

3 cups chicken stock

2 cups green peas

4 roasted red peppers (bottled)

4 saffron sprigs

Salt and pepper to taste

SERVES 4

In a glass jar, combine the oil and garlic and let sit at least 2 hours to blend the flavors. Cut the chicken breasts into ½-inch strips and pound lightly with the textured side of the meat tenderizer. Brush the strips lightly with the garlic oil, dredge in flour, and set aside.

In a large, heavy skillet, heat ⅓ cup garlic oil over medium heat. Add the green pepper and onion and sauté about 7–8 minutes. Add the chorizo and cook until lightly browned, about 4–5 minutes. Add the chicken strips and brown on both sides, about 3–4 minutes on each side, adding more garlic oil, if needed. Stir in the stock, peas, roasted peppers, saffron, salt, and pepper and bring to a boil. Lower heat to medium and simmer to reduce, about 5–10 minutes. Serve immediately with yellow rice and a green salad.

NOTE: Any extra garlic oil can be stored in the refrigerator for 2 weeks.

A popular chicken dish named for an interior region of western Spain incorporates the favorite flavors of that country. It is further highlighted with the addition of the world's most expensive spice—saffron.

Poulet Basquaise

Café Un Deux Trois, courtesy of Luis Gonzalez

¾ cup olive oil

3 (3-pound) whole chickens,
   each cut into 8 pieces

1 pound red bell peppers,
   cut in 1-inch dice

1 pound green bell peppers,
   cut in 1-inch dice

1 pound onions, cut in 1-inch dice

1½-pound Jambón de Paris

1 teaspoon crushed red pepper

6 pounds ripe tomatoes,
   seeded and chopped

5 fresh thyme sprigs

3 bay leaves

Salt and freshly ground pepper to taste

SERVES 8

In a large, heavy skillet, heat the oil over high heat. Add the chicken in three or four batches and cook until brown and crisp on all sides. Remove chicken to a platter and set aside. Pour off three-fourths of the fat from the skillet. Add bell peppers, onions, ham, and crushed red pepper to the skillet. Return to medium-low heat and cook for 10 minutes, stirring occasionally. Place skillet ingredients in a large Dutch oven, stir in the tomatoes, add the chicken, and bring to a boil. Reduce heat to medium. Add thyme, bay leaves, salt, and pepper and simmer, stirring often, until sauce thickens, about 30–40 minutes. Skim off excess fat from surface. Serve with white rice and warm, crispy French bread.

Ham, a popular ingredient in Basque cuisine, is a delicious complement to this chicken dish, rich with a variety of vegetables and herbs. If Jambón de Paris is not readily available, any good-quality ham will work.

Chicken Tikka Masala

Purnima, courtesy of Vikas Khanna

MARINADE FOR CHICKEN
2–3-inch piece fresh ginger, peeled
4 cloves garlic
1 teaspoon salt
½ teaspoon red chili powder

½ teaspoon garam masala
Juice of 1 lemon
1½ cups plain yogurt, divided
¼ cup vegetable oil
4 (4–6-ounce) boneless, skinless chicken
    breasts, cut into 1½-inch cubes

SERVES 4

In a mini-food processor, process ginger and garlic until a paste forms.

In a large nonreactive bowl, thoroughly combine the ginger/garlic paste with the salt, chili powder, garam masala, lemon juice, yogurt, and oil. Add the chicken cubes and mix well until the chicken is evenly coated. Marinate in the refrigerator overnight.

On a stovetop grill, cook chicken over medium-high heat, browning all sides, about 10–12 minutes total.

{ Luscious chunks of chicken are marinated in spices and yogurt and then simmered in a tomato and cream sauce to create an authentic Indian meal. }

TOMATO-CREAM SAUCE

1 tablespoon unsalted butter

1 clove garlic, minced

2 teaspoons ground cumin

2 teaspoons paprika

2 tablespoons dried fenugreek leaves

1 (8-ounce) can tomato sauce

¼ cup tomato paste

1½ cups heavy cream

Salt

⅓ cup sweetened coconut
   flakes to garnish

In a large, heavy skillet, melt the butter over medium heat and sauté the garlic for 1 minute. Stir in the cumin, paprika, and fenugreek and cook until fragrant, about 2 minutes. Add the tomato sauce, tomato paste and cream and bring just to a boil. Reduce heat to low and simmer 20 minutes, until the sauce thickens. Add the grilled chicken cubes and simmer for 10–12 minutes. Season to taste with salt. Transfer to a decorative platter, sprinkle with coconut and serve immediately with basmati rice and naan.

Love Me Tenders with Honey-Mustard Sauce

Ellen's Stardust Diner, courtesy of Brian Heyman

HONEY-MUSTARD SAUCE
¾ cup Dijon mustard
¼ cup honey
½ teaspoon cayenne pepper

CHICKEN
4 (4–6-ounce) chicken breasts
Salt and pepper to taste
1½ cups flour
3 eggs, beaten
3–4 cups panko breadcrumbs
1 cup vegetable oil

SERVES 4

Mix together all sauce ingredients and chill. The sauce will keep in the refrigerator for 3–4 days.

Cut each breast into 1-inch diagonal pieces and gently pound to ½-inch thickness. Pat dry and season with salt and pepper. Coat the chicken strips with flour and dip into the beaten eggs. Finally, thoroughly coat with panko.

In a large, heavy skillet, heat the oil over medium-high heat. Add chicken strips in batches and fry until golden brown, about 2–4 minutes on each side. Drain on paper towels and serve with the sauce.

{ Chicken strips coated with panko and deep-fried are a hit for any party. Some report Elvis sightings while munching on them. }

Chicken Catupiri

Brazil Brazil, courtesy of Ernane Sardinha

4 (6–8-ounce) chicken breasts
Salt and pepper to taste
2 cups sautéed spinach
4 sticks catupiri cheese, ½ x 3 inches
¼ cup flour

Vegetable oil for frying
2 tablespoons unsalted butter
2 tablespoons lemon juice
½ cup chicken stock
½ cup dry white wine

SERVES 4

Gently pound the chicken breasts to a uniform flatness and season with salt and pepper.

Divide the spinach among the breasts and spread evenly. Place 1 stick catupiri on top of the spinach and carefully roll up, wide end to narrow end, and secure with a toothpick. Lightly coat with flour.

In a large, deep skillet, heat 1½ inches oil over medium heat to 350 degrees. Fry the chicken rolls until golden brown, about 5–6 minutes on each side. Remove and drain on paper towels. Pour off excess oil from the skillet. Return to heat; add butter, lemon juice, stock, and wine. Bring to a boil and then reduce heat to medium-low. Place chicken rolls in the skillet and simmer 15–20 minutes, or until chicken reaches a temperature of 160 degrees. Serve with mashed potatoes and crusty Portuguese bread.

Catupiri is a soft, mild cheese, widely used in Brazil and available in specialty stores. Philadelphia cream cheese can be substituted if catupiri is not readily available.

Chicken Hash

'21' Club, courtesy of John Greeley

MORNAY SAUCE

4 tablespoons unsalted butter

4 tablespoons flour

1/2 cup dry white wine

1/2 cup hot chicken stock

2 cups warm heavy cream

4 cups grated Gruyère cheese

1/2 cup grated Parmesan cheese

1 teaspoon nutmeg

Pinch of cayenne pepper

Salt to taste

1 egg yolk, beaten

CHICKEN AND PLATING

4 cups cooked and cooled 1/2-
inch dice chicken breast

1 cup grated Parmesan cheese

2 cups cooked wild rice

2 cups cooked spinach

SERVES 4

To make the sauce, in a large, heavy saucepan, whisk butter
and flour over low heat about 2–3 minutes, taking care not
to brown. Gradually whisk in wine, hot chicken stock and
warm cream. Raise heat and bring the sauce to a boil. Remove
from heat and whisk in cheeses until melted and well blended.
Season with nutmeg, pepper and salt. In a small bowl, add 1/2
cup sauce to the egg yolk. Pour back into the saucepan.

In a large, heavy skillet, over medium heat, add the chicken
and stir in half of the sauce. Gradually add the remaining sauce
and heat until bubbly. Top with the Parmesan cheese and place
under the broiler to melt and lightly brown the cheese. Divide
the rice among plates and make a well in the middle of each.
Circle each rice ring with spinach. Scoop the piping hot hash
into the rice rings and serve immediately.

A mornay sauce is basically a béchamel sauce
enriched with Gruyère and Parmesan cheeses.
This hash calls for cooked chicken, so leftovers
can be briefly heated in the sauce to create an
elegant dinner.

seafood

Crabcakes with Chipotle Remoulade Sauce

Sardi's, courtesy of Patrick Pinon

CRABCAKES

1 tablespoon butter

1¼ tablespoons each finely diced
onion, celery, red bell pepper,
and green bell pepper

1 cup fresh white breadcrumbs

¾ cup Hellmann's mayonnaise

¼ cup finely chopped scallions

¼ cup finely chopped Italian parsley

3 teaspoons Pommery or
stone-ground mustard

½ teaspoon Old Bay seasoning

½ teaspoon Louisiana hot sauce

¼ teaspoon Worcestershire sauce

¼ teaspoon Colman's Mustard Powder

1 pound fresh jumbo lump crabmeat

SERVES 4

In a small skillet, heat butter over medium heat. Add onion, celery, and bell peppers and lightly sauté about 1–2 minutes. Place in a large mixing bowl and add all remaining crabcake ingredients except crabmeat and blend well. Gently fold in crabmeat.

Mix breadcrumbs and cornmeal well. Using an ice cream scoop, shape crabmeat mixture into 8 patties. Roll the crabcakes in the coating mixture to lightly coat.

In a large, heavy skillet, heat 1 tablespoon olive oil over medium heat. Add crabcakes in batches and sauté, adding more olive oil as needed, until golden brown on both sides, about 4–5 minutes on one side and 3–4 minutes on the other side. Place on a warm platter and keep warm in a 150–170-degree oven.

Succulent jumbo lump crabmeat, seasoned to perfection with an array of spices, is further enhanced by the kick of chipotle chili (dried jalapeño) in adobo sauce.

COATING

1 cup fresh breadcrumbs
½ cup coarse yellow cornmeal
Olive oil for sautéing

CHIPOTLE REMOULADE SAUCE

5 cloves garlic, peeled
Juice of 1 lime
⅓ cup olive oil

1 tablespoon butter
1 tomato, peeled, seeded, and diced
⅓ cup finely chopped onion
1 teaspoon tomato paste
Pinch of ground cumin
Pinch of ground coriander
¼ cup chopped cilantro
1 chipotle chile in adobo sauce
½ cup Hellmann's mayonnaise

To make the remoulade, boil garlic in water in a small saucepan until softened, about 2–3 minutes. Transfer to a blender and puree with lime juice and olive oil.

In a small skillet, heat the butter over medium heat. Add tomato and onion and sauté about 2–3 minutes. Add tomato paste, cumin, coriander, cilantro, and chile. Blend well and cook about 1–2 minutes. Set aside to cool. When cooled, fold in mayonnaise. Serve with the warm crabcakes.

This delicate-flavored but meaty fish achieved royal status when England's King Edward II declared that all sturgeon caught had to be offered to the king. Here it is crowned with its own roe, often referred to as the true caviar.

Caviar-Crowned Sturgeon

Russian Tea Room, courtesy of Marc Taxiera

1¼ pounds parsnips, diced

1 quart whole milk

2 vanilla pods, cut in half

16 pieces baby fennel, thoroughly washed

3 whole black peppercorns

2 star anise

1 cinnamon stick

1 teaspoon ground cumin

4 cups orange juice

Salt and pepper to taste

2 tablespoons canola oil

4 (6-ounce) sturgeon fillets,
about 1 inch thick

4 tablespoons unsalted butter

4 ounces sevruga caviar

SERVES 4

Place the parsnips, milk, and vanilla pods in a heavy saucepan. Add water, if needed, to cover the parsnips. Bring to a boil and then immediately reduce heat to medium-low; simmer 20–30 minutes until parsnips are tender. Strain the parsnips, reserving the cooking liquid, and remove the pods. In a blender, puree the parsnips until smooth, adding a little cooking liquid, if necessary. Set aside and keep warm.

In a heavy saucepan, place fennel, peppercorns, star anise, cinnamon stick, and cumin. Cover with the orange juice and bring to a boil. Reduce heat to very low, cover, and cook for 10–15 minutes. Remove fennel and continue to reduce sauce another 5–7 minutes. Strain, season with salt and pepper, and keep warm.

Preheat oven to 350 degrees.

In a large, heavy, ovenproof skillet, heat the oil over medium heat. Sear the fish until golden brown, about 2–3 minutes on each side. Place fish in the oven, cover lightly with foil and cook until opaque, about 6–8 minutes. Remove from oven and top each fillet with 1 tablespoon butter. Spread the parsnip puree equally in the center of each plate, leaving 2-inch rims around the edge. Place 4 braised fennel pieces on the puree. Place the fillets on top and dollop with caviar. Drizzle the spiced orange juice sauce over the fish and fennel-topped puree.

Camarao con Coco

Brazil Brazil, courtesy of Ernane Sardinha

2 pounds jumbo shrimp
Juice of 2 limes
Salt and freshly ground pepper to taste
2 tablespoons olive oil
1 tablespoon unsalted butter
½ cup chopped onion
2 cloves garlic, minced
1 cup chopped shiitake mushrooms

¼ cup brandy
1 cup coconut milk
1 cup coconut water, mixed with
    1 teaspoon cornstarch
½ cup heavy cream
¼ cup chopped cilantro
¼ cup chopped parsley to garnish

SERVES 4

Marinate the shrimp in the lime juice, salt and pepper.

In a large, heavy skillet, heat the oil and butter over medium heat and sauté the onion and garlic for about 2–3 minutes. Add the mushrooms and sauté for 3 minutes. Add the brandy and cook for 1 minute. Stir in the coconut milk, coconut water mixture, and heavy cream; bring to a boil. Add the shrimp and cilantro and boil, stirring constantly, another 2–3 minutes, or until the sauce thickens to desired consistency. Season to taste with salt and pepper.

Sprinkle with parsley and serve immediately.

Sweet, succulent shrimp are cooked in a luscious sauce of brandy, coconut milk, coconut water, and heavy cream. For impressive presentation, it can be served to each guest in a half coconut shell.

Tilapia with Crabmeat Dressing

Brazil Brazil, courtesy of Ernane Sardinha

CRABMEAT DRESSING

3 tablespoons palm oil

1/3 cup chopped red bell pepper

1/3 cup chopped green bell pepper

1/3 cup chopped onion

1 tablespoon chopped ginger

1 pound crabmeat

1/4 cup plain breadcrumbs

1 cup coconut milk

FISH

4 (7–9-ounce) tilapia fillets

Salt and pepper to taste

SAUCE

1/2 cup dry white wine

4 tablespoons unsalted butter

Juice from 1 lemon

1 teaspoon saffron

Salt and pepper to taste

SERVES 4

Preheat oven to 350 degrees.

In a large, heavy skillet, heat the oil over medium heat. Add the peppers, onion, and ginger and sauté for 4 minutes. Fold in the crabmeat and breadcrumbs. Add the coconut milk and heat through, about 2–3 minutes. Place the dressing in a bowl and set aside for 10 minutes.

Season the tilapia with salt and pepper. On a lightly buttered baking sheet, divide the dressing into four servings. Top each with a tilapia fillet and bake until tilapia is opaque, about 15 minutes.

While fish is baking, place all of the sauce ingredients in a saucepan and simmer over medium-low heat for 5–7 minutes. Plate each crabmeat-dressed tilapia, nap with sauce, and serve immediately.

Palm oil is a popular cooking oil in African and Brazilian cuisine. While it is high in saturated fat, its distinctive flavor gives great richness to this seafood combo. Indulge!

Seared Sea Scallops on Spinach Beds

Pergola Des Artistes, courtesy of Jean-Christian Ponsolle

2 pounds dry-packed sea
  scallops (about 30–32)
2 tablespoons olive oil
Juice of 1 lemon
1 teaspoon chopped shallots
½ teaspoon fresh finely chopped thyme
Salt and pepper to taste

SPINACH
2 tablespoons olive oil
6 cloves garlic, finely chopped
2 (10-ounce) bags fresh spinach
Salt and pepper to taste

SERVES 6–8

In a nonreactive bowl, combine the scallops, oil, lemon juice, shallots, thyme, salt, and pepper. Set aside at room temperature.

In a Dutch oven, heat 2 tablespoons oil over medium heat. Sauté garlic for 1 minute. Add spinach and sauté about 3–4 minutes, or until wilted. Season with salt and pepper. Set aside and keep warm.

Heat a large, heavy skillet on medium-high until hot. Do not add oil. Add scallops in batches (do not crowd) and sear for 2 minutes, or until browned. Turn and cook 30 seconds. Divide spinach among plates, top with 4 or 5 scallops each, and serve.

When purchasing scallops, be sure they are not white but rather off-white or light beige. White scallops have been soaked in water to increase their weight, thus, increasing the cost. Find a fishmonger you can trust.

Mustard-Crusted Salmon with Mustard Beurre Blanc

Algonquin Hotel, courtesy of Alex Aubry

MUSTARD BEURRE BLANC

2 shallots, minced

1 cup dry white wine

¼ cup fresh lemon juice

1 sprig fresh rosemary

1 sprig fresh thyme

1½ sticks unsalted butter, room temperature

1 tablespoon Dijon mustard

Salt and white pepper to taste

SALMON

4 (6–8-ounce) salmon fillets

½ cup Dijon mustard

1–1½ cups panko breadcrumbs

2 tablespoons olive oil

Lemon wedges and coarsely chopped Italian parsley to garnish

SERVES 4

In a nonreactive saucepan, combine shallots, wine, lemon juice, rosemary, and thyme and heat over high heat. Continue stirring and reduce to 2 tablespoons. Remove rosemary and thyme. Lower heat and gradually whisk butter into saucepan until sauce emulsifies. Blend in Dijon mustard and season with salt and pepper. Keep warm while the salmon cooks.

Rub both sides of salmon fillets with Dijon mustard. Coat with panko, lightly pressing into the mustard coating.

In a large, heavy, nonstick skillet, heat the oil over medium-high heat. Carefully add fillets and sear 4–5 minutes on the first side and 2–3 minutes on the second side, or until golden brown and pink in the middle. Plate and garnish with lemon wedges and parsley and serve with the Mustard Beurre Blanc on the side.

Beurre Blanc, meaning "white butter," is a classic French sauce. It combines white wine, fresh herbs, and lemon juice and is given extra zip with the addition of Dijon mustard.

Shrimp Enchilada

Iguana, courtesy of Terry Wicks

3 tablespoons olive oil

2 cloves garlic, minced

2 pounds jumbo shrimp, finely diced

¼ cup chopped cilantro

Salt and pepper to taste

½ cup fresh or frozen corn, thawed

½ cup chopped tomatoes

½ cup chopped onions

1 cup dry white wine

1 cup heavy cream

¼ cup mayonnaise

8 (8-inch) flour tortillas

SERVES 4

In a large, heavy skillet, heat the oil over medium-high heat. Add garlic and sauté for 2–3 minutes. Add shrimp, cilantro, salt, and pepper and cook 2–3 minutes, or until shrimp is opaque. Stir in the corn, tomatoes, onions, and wine, lower heat to medium, and reduce for 5–10 minutes. Add the cream and mayonnaise and simmer until desired consistency. Serve with warm flour tortillas on the side and allow guests to create their own enchiladas, whether rolled or layered.

Don't confuse enchilada with enchilado, a semi-hard to hard cheese originating in Mexico. Enchilada is a Mexican specialty that, in this recipe, uses flour tortillas to encase a scrumptious shrimp filling.

Salmao a Brazileira

Brazil Brazil, courtesy of Ernane Sardinha

3 tablespoons butter

2 cloves garlic, minced

¾ cup passion fruit juice

¾ cup heavy cream

¾ cup fish stock or clam juice

2 tablespoons Dijon mustard

4 (8-ounce) salmon steaks

Salt and pepper to taste

2 lemons

3 tablespoons olive oil

2 tablespoons butter

SERVES 4

In a heavy saucepan, heat butter over medium heat. Add garlic and sauté for 2–3 minutes. Stir in the juice, cream, stock, and mustard. Bring to a boil, then lower heat to medium-low and reduce for 10–15 minutes, stirring constantly. Sauce should reduce to about 1½ cups.

Season salmon steaks with salt and pepper and drizzle lemon juice on both sides.

In a large, heavy skillet, heat the oil and butter over high heat. Cook the salmon on one side about 4–5 minutes. Turn and cook about 2–3 minutes more. Plate and spoon sauce over each steak. Serve with Brazilian Collard Greens (see page 180).

If flying to Brazil is not in your immediate plans, you can still escape for an evening with this delectable dish. Salmon fillets are pan-seared and topped with an easy-to-make tropical sauce of passion fruit juice and heavy cream that guests will believe took hours.

"While I have produced countless television shows and documentaries, I have also done my share in the theater. One of my most memorable exploits was creating the first ever U.S./Russian co-production of a Broadway musical. We brought the cast of *Sophisticated Ladies* to Moscow and we were thrilled to have it sold out for the two-week run. Then, we learned there was no translation for 'sophisticated' in Russian, so the show was promoted as *Ladies of the Evening*. Nancy Reagan and Raisa Gorbachev were the co-chairs for opening night!"

—Lucy Jarvis, Executive Producer

Trout Amandine

Le Rivage, courtesy of Paul Denamiel

1 cup milk
Salt and pepper to taste
4 (6–8-ounce) trout fillets
Flour for dredging

6 tablespoons unsalted butter, divided
½ cup sliced almonds
Chopped parsley and lemon
  slices to garnish

SERVES 4

In a large bowl, combine milk, salt, and pepper. Dry trout fillets with paper towels, soak in milk for 3 minutes, and then dredge in flour.

In a large, heavy skillet, heat 4 tablespoons butter over medium heat. Add trout fillets and sauté on each side about 3–4 minutes, or until golden brown. While fillets are cooking, heat remaining butter in a small skillet. Add almonds and sauté until lightly browned. Plate fillets and pour almond sauce over each. Sprinkle with parsley and serve with lemon slices.

This ever-popular fish dish receives its name from its rich, buttery almond sauce. Amandine is also a French name for a girl, meaning "lovable," and can surely be applied to this entrée.

Black Sea Bass with Potatoes, Asparagus, and Citrus Dressing

Lucille's Grill at B.B. King, courtesy of Master Chef Erik Blauberg

CITRUS DRESSING

½ teaspoon salt

2 teaspoons each fresh
  lemon and lime juice

3 tablespoons olive oil

4 teaspoons grape seed oil

Finely grated zest each of ¼
  lemon, ¼ lime, ¼ orange

Pinch of fresh grated ginger

FISH AND VEGETABLES

4 (7-ounce) black bass fillets, skin on

Sea salt and freshly ground white pepper

6 tablespoons olive oil, divided

2 tablespoons grapeseed oil

8 fingerling potatoes, blanched
  and cut in ¼-inch slices

4 white asparagus, blanched and cut in
  1-inch slices (8 minute cooking time)

4 green asparagus, blanched and cut in
  1-inch slices (5½ minute cooking time)

½ cup quartered chanterelle mushrooms,
  sautéed with 1 tablespoon butter and
  2 tablespoons chopped shallots

Salt and pepper to taste

2 tablespoons thinly sliced chives

SERVES 4

To make the dressing, dissolve the salt in the citrus juices. Gradually whisk in the oils. Finally, whisk in the zests and ginger. Set aside.

Dry the bass with paper towels and season with salt and pepper. In two large, heavy skillets, heat 3 tablespoons oil in each over medium-high heat. When oil begins to smoke, place 2 fillets skin side down in each skillet. Cook until the skin is crispy, about 4 minutes, then turn fillets over and cook 15 seconds. Remove from pan, blot excess oil, set aside and keep warm.

In a separate skillet, heat the grapeseed oil over medium heat. Add the potatoes, asparagus, and mushrooms. Season to taste with salt and pepper and stir in the chives. Divide the vegetables in the centers of 4 plates, place 1 bass fillet on top and drizzle the dressing around and on top of the fish. Serve immediately.

A true bass, black bass is quickly pan-seared, placed on a bed of mixed vegetables, and drizzled with a refreshing three-citrus fruit sauce.

Crevettes Provençales

Le Petit Café Un Deux Trois, courtesy of Michele Blanes

2 tablespoons olive oil
4 cloves garlic, thinly sliced
¼ cup finely chopped parsley

1 pound (16–20 count) extra-large shrimp
Salt and freshly ground pepper to taste

SERVES 2-4

In a large, heavy skillet, heat oil over medium-high heat. Add garlic and parsley and cook for 30–45 seconds, stirring constantly. Add the shrimp and sauté 2–2½ minutes. To prevent drying, do not overcook. Season to taste with salt and pepper. Serve immediately with crusty French bread.

Garlic plays a large role in the cuisine of Provence, France, and in this delicious dish, shrimp are quickly sautéed in a garlic sauce that takes just minutes to prepare.

Also known as St. Peter's fish, sweet-flavored tilapia is dressed with an eggplant/olive sauce that combines a variety of ingredients so popular in Mediterranean cuisine.

Chilean Tilapia with Eggplant and Olive Sauce

Patsy's, courtesy of Sal Scognamillo

EGGPLANT AND OLIVE SAUCE
½ pound small Italian eggplants,
  peeled and cut into ½-inch cubes
½ cup extra virgin olive oil, divided
8 cloves garlic, minced
1 medium red bell pepper, thinly sliced
2 tablespoons chopped fresh basil
2 anchovy fillets in oil, drained
  and finely chopped
2 tablespoons small capers,
  rinsed and drained
16–20 kalamata olives, pitted and sliced
2–3 tablespoons chopped Italian parsley

1 (14-ounce) can plum tomatoes with juice
¾ cup water
Salt and freshly ground pepper to taste

TILAPIA
4 (6–8-ounce) tilapia fillets,
  about 1½ inches thick
2–3 tablespoons unsalted butter
½ cup fish broth
Juice of 1 lemon
½ teaspoon paprika
Fresh basil leaves to garnish

SERVES 4

Preheat the oven to 450 degrees.

Toss the eggplant cubes in ¼ cup oil. Place in one layer in a baking dish and roast for 14–16 minutes, turning once. Remove from oven and set aside.

In a large, heavy, nonstick skillet, heat remaining oil over low heat. Sauté the garlic until golden brown, about 2–3 minutes. Stir in the bell pepper, basil, anchovies, capers, olives, parsley, and eggplant. Sauté for an additional 2–3 minutes. Add the tomatoes with juice and water and bring to a boil. Cover, reduce heat to low, and simmer until all ingredients are incorporated and flavors blended, about 12–15 minutes. Season to taste with salt and pepper and keep warm over low heat.

Place the fish in a baking dish and dot with butter. Pour the broth and lemon juice over top and sprinkle with paprika. Bake for 16–18 minutes. Spoon two-thirds of the sauce onto a decorative serving platter, place fish on top and spoon remaining sauce over the fish. Garnish with the basil and serve immediately with hot Italian bread.

Grilled Atlantic Salmon

Chez Josephine, courtesy of Frank Diaz

2 carrots, julienned

2 green zucchini, julienned

2 turnips, julienned

4 (6–8-ounce) skinless salmon
   fillets, 1 inch thick

Olive oil

Salt and pepper to taste

Garlic powder to taste

1 teaspoon olive oil

1 lemon

SERVES 4

Cook julienned vegetables separately in boiling salted water for 60 seconds. Strain and immediately cool by plunging into ice water. Drain and place on a paper towel. Rub the salmon fillets with oil, season with salt, pepper and garlic powder. Lightly oil a stovetop grill and place over medium heat. Grill salmon on one side for 3–4 minutes, flip and continue to grill for 4–6 minutes.

In a nonstick skillet, heat 1 teaspoon olive oil, add vegetables, and heat through, about 1 minute. Divide the vegetables among plates, drizzle with lemon juice, and top each with a salmon fillet.

Simply grilled with fresh julienned vegetables, this dish is definitely not simple in taste. And, healthy and light, it makes for the perfect spring or summer dinner.

Zuppa Di Pesce Adriatica

La Rivista, courtesy of Luciano Marchignoli

2 tablespoons olive oil

3 cloves garlic, minced

1 cup finely chopped onion

1/4 cup chopped parsley

1 cup dry white wine

1 cup water

1 pound peeled tomatoes

1 pound squid, cut into 1/2-inch rings

1 pound sole fillet, 1–1 1/2-inch chunks

1 pound striped bass, 1–1 1/2-inch chunks

1 pound white fish (whiting, red snapper, monkfish, turbot), 1–1 1/2-inch chunks

4 large shrimp, cleaned and peeled

4 littleneck clams

8 mussels

Salt and pepper to taste

1/4 cup finely chopped parsley to garnish

SERVES 4

In a large soup pot, heat the oil over medium-high heat. Add garlic, onion, and parsley and cook, stirring occasionally, about 4–5 minutes. Add wine and reduce for about 6–8 minutes. Stir in water, tomatoes, and squid. Cook over medium-high heat until boiling.

Add the sole, bass, and white fish and cook for 5 minutes. Stir in the shrimp, clams, and mussels and cook until clams and mussels open, about 5 minutes. Discard any clams or mussels that do not open. Ladle into large soup bowls and serve with crusty country bread.

Seven kinds of seafood are used in this substantial Italian fish soup, traditionally served on Christmas Eve. This bounty of seafood is also referred to as "The Feast of the Seven Fishes."

Moules Mariniere

Le Rivage, courtesy of Paul Denamiel

1 gallon mussels, cleaned and debearded
1 tablespoon butter
2 shallots, minced

1 cup dry white wine
2 tablespoons chopped parsley
2 cloves garlic, minced

SERVES 4

Place mussels, butter, shallots, and wine in a large pot. Steam uncovered over high heat, stirring occasionally, until mussels open. Discard any mussels that do not open. When open, remove mussels from pot, set aside, and keep warm. Strain liquid, return to pot, and reduce over medium-high heat about 4–5 minutes. Pour over mussels and sprinkle with parsley and garlic. Serve with fresh crusty French bread.

Mussels cooked in white wine is said to be prepared *a la mariniere*, French for "mariner's style." This easy-to-make dish truly captures the fresh taste and smell of the sea.

meats & game

Steak Tartare

Pergola Des Artistes, courtesy of Jean-Christian Ponsolle

1 pound hand-chopped sirloin
1 egg yolk
2 tablespoons olive oil
1 tablespoon Tabasco sauce
1 tablespoon Worcestershire sauce
1 teaspoon finely chopped shallots

1 teaspoon capers
1/2 teaspoon Dijon mustard
1/2 teaspoon ketchup
1/2 teaspoon chopped cornichon
Crusty French bread, toasted

SERVES 4

Place hand-chopped sirloin in a large bowl. Slightly flatten with back of a cooking spoon and make indentation in center of meat. Drop egg yolk in indentation and drizzle oil over meat. Add remaining ingredients and fold together until well incorporated. Serve with French bread.

Believed to go back to medieval times in Russia, when Tatars shredded and ate raw meat, this seasoned raw beef has retained its popularity through the centuries. When choosing the beef, be sure to purchase from a reputable butcher.

Polenta e Cinghiale (Wild Boar and Polenta)

Trattoria Dopo Teatro, courtesy of Roberto Lamonte

BOAR

1 pound wild boar shoulder meat,
   cut into 1-inch chucks
2 carrots, diced
1 stalk celery, chopped
1 onion, diced
1 clove garlic, minced
½ cup fresh rosemary
½ cup fresh sage

3 cups dry red wine
½ cup olive oil
1 (28-ounce) can crushed tomatoes
1 cup water
Salt and pepper to taste

POLENTA

1 cup yellow cornmeal
Coarsely chopped Italian parsley to garnish

SERVES 4–6

In a large nonreactive bowl, combine the meat, carrots, celery, onion, garlic, herbs, and wine; cover and refrigerate for 24 hours. To cook, remove the boar from the marinade and set aside. Strain the vegetables and herbs and reserve the wine.

In a Dutch oven, heat the oil over medium heat and sauté the vegetables and herbs for 5 minutes. Add boar meat and cook until browned. Add the wine and cook until the wine evaporates. Add the tomatoes, 1 cup water, salt, and pepper. Lower heat and simmer 1½–2 hours.

To make the polenta, boil 2 cups salted water. Add the cornmeal. Remove from heat, cover, and allow to thicken, about 4–5 minutes. Divide the polenta among plates, top with boar, and sprinkle with parsley.

Wild boar, a type of wild pig, is a lean meat that is best cooked at a low temperature. Here it is simmered in red wine with fresh herbs to create the perfect meal for a brisk autumn or cold winter night.

Steak au Poivre

Le Rivage, courtesy of Paul Denamiel

4 tablespoons green peppercorns, divided
3 tablespoons butter
3 tablespoons olive oil
4 tablespoons dried green
   peppercorns, divided

4 (6–8-ounce) well marbled strip
   steaks, 1½ inches thick
¼ cup cognac
¼ cup crème fraîche
Salt to taste

SERVES 4

Preheat oven to 175 degrees F.

Lightly crush 2 tablespoons peppercorns and rub on steaks. In a large, heavy skillet, heat the butter and oil over medium-high heat. Add steaks and cook on each side, about 4–5 minutes for medium-rare. Place in a warm oven while preparing sauce. Pour off excess fat from skillet and return to medium heat. Stir in cognac and flambé. Add crème fraîche, remaining peppercorns, and salt and boil about 1–2 minutes. Plate steaks and spoon sauce over each. Serve with French fries or grilled tomatoes.

This traditional French peppered steak flambéed with cognac and enriched with crème fraîche is a hearty dish that will delight any steak lover.

Steak Fiorentina

Bistecca Fiorentina, courtesy of Luciano Marchignoli

TUSCAN SALSA

3 tablespoons olive oil

1 cup dry white wine

4 sage leaves

2 cloves garlic, minced

2 tablespoons chopped fresh rosemary

1/2 cup finely chopped Italian parsley

STEAK

1 (50-ounce) porterhouse
steak, 2 inches thick

Salt and pepper to taste

SERVES 2

Combine salsa ingredients and set aside 2–3 hours to allow flavors to blend.

Broil steak on each side, about 9–10 minutes for rare, 10–12 minutes for medium-rare, or 12–14 minutes for medium. While steaks are cooking, baste occasionally with Tuscan Salsa. Allow steak to sit for 5 minutes to redistribute juices. Slice and serve with French fries and a green salad.

No, your eyes do not deceive you. Yes, Luciano Serves a 50-ounce porterhouse for two people. But a light touch is added with a refreshing white wine-and-herb salsa. It's no shame to ask for a doggie bag.

Strawberry-Sauced Filet Mignon

Brazil Brazil, courtesy of Ernane Sardinha

STRAWBERRY SAUCE
4 teaspoons sugar
4 tablespoons unsalted butter
1 cup sliced fresh strawberries
½ cup red wine

½ cup beef stock
4 (10-ounce) filet mignon
Canola oil
Salt and pepper to taste

SERVES 4

In a large, heavy saucepan, heat the sugar with 1 teaspoon water over medium-high heat until caramelized, about 3–4 minutes. Stir constantly with a wooden spoon to prevent burning. Add the butter and strawberries and gently blend. Add wine and flambé. Stir in the stock, bring to a boil, and immediately reduce heat to medium-low. While the sauce simmers for 10 minutes, heat a stovetop grill over medium-high heat. Lightly brush filets with oil and season with salt and pepper. Grill the filets for 4–5 minutes on each side for medium-rare. Plate and top with the sauce.

Chicken, duck, and pork chops are often paired with fruits for a great flavor contrast. Here filet mignon is adorned with an unusual but delicious strawberry/red wine sauce. Serve with mashed potatoes and Brazilian Collard Greens (see page 180).

Petit Fillet of Beef with Tarragon Cognac Mustard Sauce

Sardi's, courtesy of Patrick Pinon

2 tablespoons canola oil
6 tablespoons butter, divided
4 (6-ounce) center-cut beef fillets,
    about 1½ inches thick
Salt and pepper to taste
¼ cup cognac
2 tablespoons olive oil

2 cloves garlic, minced
1 cup Chardonnay
3 cups heavy cream
1½ teaspoons Dijon mustard
1 tablespoon chopped fresh tarragon
Splash of cognac

SERVES 4

In a large, heavy skillet, heat canola oil and 2 tablespoons butter over medium-high heat. Season fillets with salt and pepper. Sauté the beef fillets about 4–5 minutes on each side for medium-rare. Remove skillet from the heat, carefully add the cognac and flambé. Remove fillets to a warm platter and keep warm.

In the same skillet, heat olive oil over medium-high heat and sauté garlic until light brown. Cool a few seconds, then add the Chardonnay. Boil for a few minutes, stirring constantly and scraping the bottom of the pan to deglaze. Add the cream, lower heat, simmer until the sauce thickens and then strain into a small saucepan. Bring to a boil and add mustard, remaining butter, tarragon, and a splash of cognac. Spoon sauce over fillets and serve.

Tender fillets of beef are napped with a classic French sauce of mustard, heavy cream and cognac to create an incredibly satisfying meal. Serve with Sautéed Julienned Portobellos (see page 171).

Spice-Rubbed Pork Chops with Port Wine and Plum Sauce

Joe Allen, courtesy of Victor Flores

SPICE BLEND

1 teaspoon each fennel seeds, coriander seeds, red pepper flakes, and sweet paprika

1/2 teaspoon ground cinnamon

PORK CHOPS

4 bone-in center-cut pork chops, 1 1/2 inches thick

3 tablespoons olive oil

Kosher salt and pepper to taste

3 tablespoons canola oil

SERVES 4

In a small sauté pan, heat the spices over low heat, stirring occasionally, until fragrant, about 10–12 minutes. Be careful not to burn. Cool the spices for 15 minutes and grind in a spice grinder.

Rub the pork chops with the olive oil. Thoroughly rub the Spice Blend over the pork chops and refrigerate a few hours or overnight. About 20 minutes before cooking, remove chops from refrigerator, season with salt and pepper, and let stand at room temperature.

Preheat the oven to 400 degrees and place a baking sheet in the oven while it is preheating.

Thick, succulent pork chops are coated with fragrant spices and marinated. Briefly sautéed and then baked, the chops are served with a sweet, fruity wine sauce.

PORT WINE AND PLUM SAUCE

4 tablespoons unsalted butter, divided

2 shallots, minced

1½ cups port wine

1 dried plum (prune), sliced

½ cup chicken stock

Salt and pepper to taste

Heat a large, heavy sauté pan over medium-high heat. When pan begins to smoke, add the canola oil and sear pork chops, about 2 minutes on each side. Discard the oil, place the chops on the preheated baking sheet, and bake for about 15–17 minutes.

To make the Plum Sauce, in the same sauté pan, heat 2 tablespoons butter over medium-high heat. Add shallots and sauté until translucent. Add the wine and dried plum and reduce until almost evaporated, about 5–10 minutes. Add the stock and reduce about 4–6 minutes. When the pork chops are almost ready, bring the sauce to a boil. Whisk in the remaining butter until sauce emulsifies. Pour sauce over chops and serve.

Berkshire Pork Chops with Apple and Cranberry Chutney

Algonquin Hotel, courtesy of Alex Aubry

2 tablespoons olive oil
4 (1½-inch-thick) Berkshire
  pork chops with bones
Sea salt and pepper to taste

CHUTNEY
2 tablespoons olive oil
¼ cup chopped onion

2 Granny Smith apples, peeled
  and cut in ½-inch dice
½ cup cranberry juice
¼ cup dried cranberries, chopped
½ cup chicken stock
1 tablespoon cornstarch

SERVES 4

Preheat oven to 350 degrees.

In a large, heavy skillet, heat the oil over medium-high heat. Season pork chops with salt and pepper. Add chops to pan and sear 1–2 minutes on each side, until brown. Remove to an ovenproof pan and roast in the oven 10–14 minutes, or until center reaches 160 degrees.

While chops are cooking, in the same skillet heat 2 tablespoons oil over medium-high heat. Sauté onion for 2–3 minutes. Add apples and sauté for 3–4 minutes, or until golden brown. Deglaze skillet with the cranberry juice and add dried cranberries. Make a slurry with the chicken stock and cornstarch and add to skillet. Lower heat and reduce until viscous. Divide the chutney among dinner plates and place 1 chop on top of each.

Berkshire pork goes back three hundred years to the herd of the House of Windsor. In Japan, it is known as Kurobuta, meaning "black hog," and is unique because of its darker color and rich, sweet flavor. Serve with wild rice and Brussels sprouts.

Do-Ahead Braised Short Ribs

Chez Josephine, courtesy of Frank Diaz

2 pounds boneless short ribs
Salt and pepper to taste
2–3 tablespoons butter

2–3 tablespoons olive oil
2 large onions, cut into 1-inch pieces
2 shallots, cut into ½-inch dice
1 stalk celery, cut into 1-inch pieces

1 carrot, cut into 1-inch pieces
1 head garlic, sliced in half widthwise
½ cup dry red wine
½ cup beef stock
2 teaspoons dry thyme
1 bay leaf
Chopped flat-leaf parsley to garnish
1 recipe Creamy Polenta (see page 174)

SERVES 4

One day in advance, season ribs with salt and pepper. In a large, heavy Dutch oven, heat butter over medium-high heat. Add ribs and cook on all sides until well browned and caramelized. Cool and refrigerate overnight.

The next day, in a large Dutch oven, heat the oil over medium-high heat. Sauté the onions, shallots, celery, and carrot until brown and caramelized. Add garlic, wine, stock, thyme, bay leaf, and ribs to Dutch oven. Bring to a boil, then lower heat and let simmer 3–4 hours. Remove ribs to a large serving dish. Strain sauce, season with salt and pepper, and pour over ribs. Garnish with parsley. Serve ribs on top of Creamy Polenta.

Who doesn't love the words "do-ahead dinner"? Ribs are simply browned a day ahead, refrigerated, and then simmered the next day with an abundance of vegetables in red wine and beef stock.

Costillas de Cordero a las Finas Hierbas

Sangria 46, courtesy of Benny Castro

16 small loin lamb chops
½ cup fresh lemon juice
4 cloves garlic, chopped
3 tablespoons olive oil
2 tablespoons fresh chopped thyme

2 tablespoons fresh chopped rosemary
1 tablespoon coarse salt
5 tablespoons coarsely crushed
    black peppercorns

SERVES 4

Rub lamb chops with lemon juice.

In a small bowl, thoroughly mix garlic and oil and liberally coat the lamb chops. Put chops in a nonreactive dish; add thyme, rosemary, salt, and pepper. Cover and refrigerate for 2 hours.

Broil lamb chops in a broiler pan, about 4 inches from the flame, for 3–4 minutes on each side for medium-rare, or 4–5 minutes on each side for well done.

Small lamb chops are marinated with lemon juice and fresh herbs and then broiled to make the ideal light springtime meal. Serve with roasted potatoes and steamed asparagus.

The Count's Stroganoff

Russian Tea Room, courtesy of Marc Taxiera

RED WINE REDUCTION

1 tablespoon olive oil
1/2 cup chopped onion
1/4 cup chopped celery
1/4 cup chopped carrots
2 cloves garlic, minced
1 1/2 bottles (750 mL) dry red wine
4 cups beef stock

CORN CREAM

2 cups corn, fresh or frozen
1 cup heavy cream
1 tablespoon fresh chopped marjoram
Salt and pepper to taste

SERVES 4

In a large, heavy stockpot, heat 1 tablespoon oil over medium-high heat. Add the onion, celery, carrots, and garlic and sauté until golden brown, about 8–10 minutes. Stir in wine and stock, lower heat and simmer until reduced to 4 cups, about 1–1 1/2 hours. Pour through a sieve into a saucepan and simmer until reduced by half. Set aside and keep warm.

In a heavy saucepan, combine corn and cream and simmer over medium heat for 10–15 minutes. Place the corn cream, marjoram, salt, and pepper in a blender and blend until semi-smooth, about the consistency of corn chowder. Place in a container, set aside and keep warm.

Not your ordinary stroganoff of beef cubes. This dish reaches royal heights with whole filet mignon and slices of foie gras and would be sure to please its namesake, Count Stroganov.

STROGANOFF

2 tablespoons plus 2 teaspoons
   olive oil, divided

3 cups wild mushrooms, coarsely chopped

1 pound tagliatelle pasta

4 (6-ounce) filet mignons

Salt and Pepper to taste

4 (½-inch) slices foie gras

In a large, heavy skillet, heat 2 tablespoons oil over medium-high heat. Add mushrooms and sauté 4–5 minutes. Stir in ½ cup corn cream sauce, reserving the rest. Set aside and keep warm.

Cook pasta according to package directions. While pasta is cooking, heat a cast-iron skillet over medium-high heat. Season filets with salt and pepper, add to skillet and cook 3–4 minutes on each side for medium-rare. While filets are cooking, heat 2 teaspoons oil over high heat in a heavy skillet. Season foie gras with salt and pepper, place in skillet and sauté 20–30 seconds on each side. The inside will be pink. Drain pasta and toss with the mushrooms and remaining cream sauce. Divide among dinner plates and top each with a filet. Place a slice of foie gras on top of each filet and drizzle with reduction. Serve immediately.

Jazz Berry Burger

Iridium Jazz Club, courtesy of Brian Heyman

RASPBERRY VINEGAR DRESSING

½ cup mayonnaise

¼ cup sour cream

2 tablespoons raspberry vinegar

White pepper to taste

BURGERS

2 pounds ground sirloin

2 tablespoons chopped cilantro

Salt and pepper to taste

2 tablespoons olive oil

4 sesame seed hamburger buns, toasted

Romaine lettuce

Ripe tomato slices

SERVES 4

Thoroughly combine dressing ingredients and chill.

Mix the ground sirloin, cilantro, salt, and pepper and form into 4 patties.

In a large, heavy skillet, heat the oil over medium-high heat. Cook hamburgers on each side for about 4–5 minutes for medium-well. Generously spread the buns with the dressing. Place a hamburger patty on each bun and top with lettuce and tomato.

Everyone loves a juicy burger, but this burger of chopped sirloin is further jazzed up with a raspberry vinegar dressing. It will turn your picnic into a festive event! Serve with French fries or potato salad.

Steak Tacos al Carbon

Iguana, courtesy of Terry Wicks

2 pounds flank steak
Canola oil
Ancho powder to taste
Salt and pepper to taste
2 tablespoons olive oil
2 cloves garlic, minced

¼ cup chopped tomato
¼ cup chopped onion
3 tablespoons chopped jalapeño chile
2 tablespoons chopped cilantro
12 (7-inch) flour tortillas, warm
2 cups grated Monterey Jack cheese

SERVES 4–6

Rub the flank steak with canola oil, ancho powder, salt, and pepper. Heat a stovetop grill over medium-high heat, and grill steak on each side for about 4–6 minutes. Remove and let rest for 10 minutes.

While the steak is resting, heat olive oil in a large, heavy skillet over medium-high heat. Add the garlic, tomato, onion, jalapeño, and cilantro and sauté 4–5 minutes. Cut steak into 1-inch cubes, add to skillet with the vegetables and mix well. Divide mixture evenly among the tortillas and then top with cheese. Roll and serve immediately.

The flavors and spices of Mexico combine to create the ultimate tacos that will make your dinner a real fiesta. The perfect accompaniment is black beans and rice.

"As a kid growing up in Brooklyn, I dreamed about crossing that bridge to Manhattan. Then, when I was in the sixth grade, I went to see Richard Kiley in *Man of La Mancha*. I was hooked and one of my favorite songs is still 'The Impossible Dream.' Broadway music always made me strong whenever I felt weak. While I never got to sing onstage, my job greeting actors, producers, and directors makes me a part of the theater world and it a part of me."

—Victor Palamo, Doorman at the Shubert Building
and "Mayor of 44th Street"

Braised Lamb Shanks with Early Artichoke, Spring Potato, and Fava Beans

Lucille's Grill at B.B. King, Master Chef Erik Blauberg

BRAISED LAMB SHANKS

6 tablespoons vegetable oil

4 lamb shanks, trimmed and
silver skin removed

Sea salt and freshly ground
black pepper to taste

4 large onions, coarsely chopped

3 large carrots, coarsely chopped

6 stalks celery, coarsely chopped

1 cup tomato paste

1 (750 mL) bottle Cabernet Sauvignon

1 (750 mL) bottle red ruby port wine

1 bouquet garni with 4 kaffir leaves
and 2 each bay leaves, rosemary
sprigs, and thyme (place in
cheesecloth and tie with a string)

SERVES 4

Preheat oven to 275 degrees.

In a large, heavy skillet, heat the oil over medium heat. Season the lamb shanks with salt and pepper. Carefully place the lamb shanks in the skillet and brown on all sides. Remove the shanks and set aside. Add the onions, carrots, and celery to the skillet. Sauté, stirring constantly, until golden brown. Stir in the tomato paste and cook 3 minutes, stirring constantly to prevent burning. Add the wines, cook for 5 minutes, and adjust salt and pepper. Place the lamb shanks in a large roasting pan and pour the vegetable/wine mixture over the shanks.

Add the bouquet garni, cover with aluminum foil and bake for 2½ hours. Remove the shanks from the pan, strain, reserve the jus, and keep warm.

Slow cooking in both sweet and dry wines produces the maximum tenderness of the lamb shanks. Served on top of a variety of vegetables, this lamb dish is a perfect dinner party meal, certain to impress.

VEGETABLES

1 tablespoon vegetable oil

6 tablespoons wood bacon, diced small

1/4 cup minced shallots

12 small pearl onions, blanched

6 tablespoons blanched and
   sliced red spring potato

6 tablespoons blanched and sliced
   creamer spring potato

1/4 cup blanched fava beans

1/4 cup blanched English peas

4 teaspoons thinly sliced chives

4 small bay leaves

4 small kaffir leaves

4 small rosemary sprigs

In a large, heavy skillet, heat the oil over medium-high heat. Add the bacon and cook for 2 minutes, or until lightly browned. Add the shallots and pearl onions, tossing lightly, and cook for 1 minute. Add the potatoes to the skillet and cook 1 minute. Mix in the fava beans and peas and cook for 1 minute. Season to taste with salt and pepper.

Remove from heat and stir in chives. Divide the vegetables in the center of four plates and place 1 lamb shank on top of each. Spoon the reserved jus over the shanks and garnish with bay leaves, kaffir leaves, and rosemary springs.

Hanger Steak with Roquefort Sauce

Maison, courtesy of Mario Urgiles

¼ cup butter
½ cup Roquefort cheese
¾ cup heavy cream

¼ cup olive oil
1 (3-pound) hanger steak
Salt and pepper to taste
½ cup sliced, toasted almonds to garnish
Smoked salt to garnish

SERVES 6

In a small, heavy saucepan, heat butter over medium heat. When melted, add Roquefort cheese and whisk for 1–2 minutes. Stir in the cream, lower heat, and simmer about 3–4 minutes. Set aside and keep warm.

In a large, heavy skillet, heat oil over high heat until nearly smoking. Season steak with salt and pepper. Add steak to pan and cook about 6–7 minutes on each side for medium-rare. Transfer steak to a warm platter and let rest 5 minutes. Thinly slice the steak, then plate it and spoon Roquefort sauce over each serving. Sprinkle with almonds and smoked salt.

Also known as butcher steak, hanger steak is a bit more tender than skirt steak and just as flavorful. Besides the delectable Roquefort sauce, the flavor is further intensified by the sprinkling of smoked salt. The dish is very nice served with Potato Gratinee (see page 174) and Haricots Verts (see page 177).

White Fallow Venison Hash

**Lucille's Grill at B.B. King,
courtesy of Master Chef Erik Blauberg**

4 tablespoons vegetable oil, divided

1¼ pounds boneless venison
saddle, cut into ¾-inch cubes

Salt and freshly ground black pepper

2 cups cooked diced potato

4 sprigs fresh thyme

¾ cup diced onion

¾ cup diced red bell pepper

2 cups venison or beef stock

½ cup heavy cream

1 teaspoon finely minced kaffir leaf

½ teaspoon orange zest

2 tablespoons finely sliced chives

SERVES 4

In a large, heavy Dutch oven, heat 2 tablespoons oil over high heat until the oil begins to smoke. Season venison with salt and pepper and add to the Dutch oven. Cook until golden brown on all sides, about 1½ minutes. Meat will be rare. Remove from pot and place on paper towels and set aside. Heat the remaining oil over high heat until it lightly smokes. Add potato and cook for 30 seconds, then add thyme and continue cooking until the potato is golden brown, about 2½ minutes. Lower the heat, add the onion and bell pepper and cook until translucent, about 1½ minutes. Season with salt and pepper. Stir in the stock and cream and cook until the sauce thickens. Add the kaffir, zest, chives, and venison. Stir to coat with sauce and serve immediately.

This hash calls for white fallow venison, which has been farmed for thousands of years. It is palatable and lower in fat and cholesterol than beef or pork but high in flavor. Serve with potato puree, sautéed spinach, and toast points.

sides

Asparagus Gratinee

Broadway Joe Steakhouse, courtesy of Luciano Marchignoli

2 pounds asparagus, trimmed and peeled
¼ cup softened butter plus more
for greasing the casserole

½–1 cup grated fresh Parmesan cheese
Lemon wedges to garnish

SERVES 4

Boil or steam the asparagus until crisp tender. Drain and plunge into ice water to stop the cooking and retain the bright green color. Grease a casserole and layer asparagus. Spread butter evenly over asparagus and sprinkle with Parmesan cheese. Place under the broiler until golden brown, about 5–10 minutes. Serve with lemon wedges.

Asparagus, a member of the lily family, brings to mind springtime. Simply dressed with butter, cheese, and lemon and gratineed, this is the ideal side dish for poultry, meat, or seafood.

Sautéed Julienned Portobellos

Sardi's, courtesy of Patrick Pinon

3 tablespoons olive oil
2 large portobello mushrooms
¼ cup dry white wine

2 tablespoons chopped parsley
Salt and pepper to taste

SERVES 4

In a large, heavy skillet, heat the oil over medium heat. Sauté mushrooms about 3–5 minutes on each side. Add wine and cook until it evaporates. Stir in parsley and season with salt and pepper. Cool for 2 minutes and cut into julienne strips.

Just a touch of white wine and basic seasonings are sufficient to bring out the dense, meaty flavor of these "grown-up" cremini mushrooms.

Rachael's Mac and Cheese

Ellen's Stardust Diner, courtesy of Brian Heyman

1 (16-ounce) package elbow macaroni
1 quart heavy cream
¼ cup roasted garlic

1 teaspoon chicken base
¼–½ cup grated Parmesan cheese

SERVES 6–8 AS A SIDE DISH

Cook macaroni according to package instructions. In a large, heavy saucepan, combine cream, garlic, chicken base, and cheese. Bring to a boil, reduce heat to low and simmer until reduced by half. Add drained macaroni to the saucepan, blend well, and simmer for 3 minutes. Serve immediately.

Everyone has their favorite recipe for this ultimate comfort food, but this version with a heavy cream reduction and roasted garlic is certain to gain many converts.

Onion Rings

Chez Josephine, courtesy of Frank Diaz

2 large Spanish onions
½ cup flour
1 teaspoon baking powder
Salt and pepper to taste

1 egg
½ cup milk
Canola oil for frying
Sea salt to taste

SERVES 4

Peel onions, cut into ¼-inch-slice rounds and separate into rings.

In a bowl, combine the flour, baking powder, salt, and pepper.

In a measuring cup, thoroughly whisk together the egg and milk. Add egg/milk mixture to the dry ingredients and blend well.

In a large, deep skillet, heat 1 inch of oil to 365 degrees. Fry onion rings in batches until golden brown, turning once to brown on both sides. Drain on paper towels and sprinkle with sea salt.

Large sweet onions, battered and crispy-fried are irresistible. If Spanish onions are not readily available, mild Bermuda onions are the perfect substitute.

Creamy Polenta

Chez Josephine, courtesy of Frank Diaz

2 cups whole milk
1 clove garlic, minced
1 teaspoon dried thyme

½ cup instant polenta
¼ cup shaved fresh Parmesan cheese
Salt and white pepper to taste

SERVES 4

Boil the milk, garlic, and thyme, being careful not to burn. Pour polenta into infused milk, lower heat, and stir constantly until creamy. Fold in cheese and blend well. Season to taste with salt and pepper.

{ This quick-as-a snap comfort food is rich with milk and cheese and is sure to please everyone. }

Potatoes Gratinee

Maison, courtesy of Mario Urgiles

3 large russet potatoes, ⅛-inch
   slices (see note)
1 cup grated Parmesan cheese

1 cup heavy cream
6 tablespoons unsalted butter
Salt and white pepper to taste

SERVES 4–6

Preheat oven to 350 degrees. Mix all ingredients in a large bowl. Lightly grease a 9-inch square ovenproof casserole with butter. Bake until potatoes are tender, cream is absorbed, and the top is golden brown, about 30–40 minutes.

NOTE: A mandoline is the easiest and quickest way to slice the potatoes.

{ A French classic, this rich dish of cheese, heavy cream, and butter definitely places it high on the "comfort food" list. Don't be afraid to indulge! }

Crushed Potatoes

Sardi's, courtesy of Patrick Pinon

2 pounds russet potatoes, 1½-inch dice
1 teaspoon salt
¼ cup olive oil

¼ cup melted unsalted butter
Sea salt and white pepper to taste
¼ cup thinly sliced scallions

SERVES 4

Place potatoes in a large saucepan and cover with water by 1 inch. Add salt and bring to a boil on high heat. Lower heat and simmer until potatoes are tender, about 20–25 minutes. Drain well, add the oil and butter and "crush," leaving some lumps of potato. Season to taste with salt and pepper. Fold in the scallions and serve immediately.

{ When you can't decide whether to have creamy or lumpy, don't settle. Get the best of both worlds. }

Sautéed Swiss Chard

Joe Allen, courtesy of Victor Flores

2 tablespoons olive oil
¾ cup chopped onion
2 cloves garlic, minced

1½ pounds Swiss chard, coarsely chopped
2 cups chicken stock
Salt and pepper to taste

SERVES 4–6

In a large, heavy, deep skillet, heat the oil over medium heat. Add onion and garlic and sauté about 3–4 minutes. Add chard by handfuls until it wilts. Stir in the stock and bring to a boil. Season with salt and pepper. Reduce heat and simmer about 10–15 minutes. Serve immediately.

{ Healthy and beautiful, this vegetable is a member of the beet family and is best cooked in the most basic way to capture all of its flavor. }

JOIN THE REVOLUTION!

A Tale of Two Cities
...the new musical

For tickets visit Telecharge.com or call 212-239-6200

Al Hirschfeld Theatre, 302 West 45th St.
TaleMusical.com

Haricots Verts

Sardi's, courtesy of Patrick Pinon

2 pounds haricots verts
4 tablespoons unsalted butter
½ cup chopped onion
2 cloves garlic, minced

2 tablespoons red wine vinegar
Salt and pepper to taste
Freshly ground nutmeg
2 tablespoons chopped parsley

SERVES 4-6

In a large pot, bring 2 quarts salted water to a boil. Add haricots verts, bring to a boil and boil for 5 minutes. Drain and plunge into a large bowl of ice water for 5 minutes. Drain and set aside.

In a large, heavy skillet, melt the butter over medium heat. Add the onion and garlic and sauté for 3 minutes. Raise heat to high, add the haricots verts and sauté for 2 minutes, stirring constantly. Add vinegar and heat for 30 seconds. Season to taste with salt and pepper. Remove to serving platter and then sprinkle with nutmeg and parsley.

French "green beans," these long, thin haricots verts are quickly blanched and sautéed until crisp-tender. Just a sprinkle of nutmeg adds that special touch.

"With the help of many people, I have been nurturing and growing Broadway Blessing, an interfaith service of song, dance and story, since 1997. Held on the second Monday of each September, its purpose is to gather people to celebrate the creative spirit and ask God's blessing for the new season. I think the artists who take part and those in the audience feel affirmed, and affirmation is otherwise hard to come by in the difficult world of the performing arts. It is an affirmation that asks nothing of them—no donation, no conversion; it's just a celebration of giftedness and a recognition of how important these creative gifts are in all of our lives."

—Retta Blaney, founder, Broadway Blessing, and theater critic, *National Catholic Reporter*

Creamed Spinach

Frankie & Johnnie's Steakhouse, courtesy of Peter Chimos

5 tablespoons olive oil, divided
2 (10-ounce) bags fresh spinach
3 tablespoons unsalted butter
1/3 cup chopped onion
3 cloves garlic, minced

3 tablespoons flour
3/4 cup heavy cream
Salt and pepper to taste
Freshly grated Parmesan
cheese (optional)

SERVES 4

In a large, heavy Dutch oven, heat 2 tablespoons oil over medium-high heat. Add spinach by handfuls and cook until coated with olive oil and wilted. Remove, squeeze out excess liquid, and set aside. Discard liquid. Heat remaining oil in the Dutch oven. Add the onion and garlic and sauté about 2–3 minutes. Stir in the flour and cook about 1–2 minutes, being careful not to let the flour brown. Whisk in the cream, reduce heat, and simmer about 4–5 minutes to slightly thicken the sauce. Fold in the cooked spinach and heat through. Season with salt and pepper. Sprinkle with Parmesan cheese, if desired.

No "old New York" steakhouse would ever dream of excluding creamed spinach from its menu, as it goes hand in hand with any type of steak.

Brazilian Collard Greens

Brazil Brazil, courtesy of Ernane Sardinha

¼ cup olive oil
½ cup chopped onion
2 cloves garlic, minced

2 pounds collard greens,
   coarsely chopped
Salt and crushed red pepper to taste
¼ cup red wine vinegar

SERVES 4

In a large, heavy, deep skillet, heat the oil over medium-high heat. Add onion and garlic and sauté about 3–4 minutes. Add greens in batches and cook until wilted. Season with salt and pepper and then sprinkle in the vinegar and toss.

Popular in Brazilian cooking, collard greens' flavor is a cross between kale and spinach. Simply sautéed, it gets extra zip from the addition of red wine vinegar.

Bubble and Squeak

P.J. Clarke's, courtesy of Mike De Fonzo

1 pound russet potatoes,
   cut in 1½-inch dice
1 teaspoon salt
¼ pound bacon, chopped
1 pound savoy cabbage, thinly sliced

½ cup chopped leeks
½ cup chopped scallions
Salt and white pepper to taste
Canola oil for frying

SERVES 4

Put potatoes in a saucepan and cover with water by 1 inch.
Add 1 teaspoon salt and bring to a boil over high heat. Reduce
heat and simmer until potatoes are tender, about 15–20
minutes.

In a large, heavy, deep skillet, cook bacon until crispy. Remove
bacon but do not discard bacon fat. Add the cabbage, leeks,
and scallions. Cover and cook over medium heat until cabbage
is tender, about 10–15 minutes. When potatoes are cooked, run
through a ricer or thoroughly mash with a hand mixer. Season
to taste with salt and pepper. Add the potatoes to the cabbage
mixture and mix well. Press down to flatten and form a cake.
Cook on medium-high heat (do not stir) until the bottom is
crusty and golden brown, about 8–10 minutes. Flip onto a
serving plate crusty side up and serve immediately.

A British tradition, this combo of potatoes and
cabbage is named for the sounds it makes
while cooking. It is hearty enough to double and
serve as an entrée with a simple green salad.

"I have many Broadway memories, from the Lamb's Club in its heyday to the commercial I made in Times Square and the days (and drinks) I spent at Sardi's Little Bar to The Bordello on 42nd Street, whose building now houses one of my favorite Theater District restaurants, Chez Josephine.

—Francis Anthony, "The Love Chef," actor, author

Crusted Broiled Tomatoes

Le Rivage, courtesy of Paul Denamiel

⅓ cup melted butter plus 1 tablespoon
   butter, room temperature
3 large beefsteak tomatoes,
   cut into 1½-inch slices

Sea salt and freshly ground back pepper
1 cup fresh breadcrumbs
2 tablespoons chopped fresh basil
2 tablespoons chopped fresh parsley

SERVES 4–6

Line a broiler pan with aluminum foil and grease with 1 table-spoon butter. Place tomatoes in a single layer on the pan and season with salt and pepper. Mix the melted butter with the breadcrumbs and sprinkle over top. Broil 5–6 inches from the flame until golden brown, about 2–4 minutes, taking care not to burn. Combine the basil and parsley. Remove tomatoes from broiler and sprinkle with the herb blend.

The season is short for vine-ripened tomatoes, so take advantage while it lasts. These are so easy to prepare and delicious when cooked, as they are still firm but slightly juicy.

Lyonnaise Potatoes

Frankie & Johnnie's Steakhouse, courtesy of Peter Chimos

5 tablespoons unsalted butter
¾ cup chopped onion
3 cups cooked and sliced white potatoes

Salt and white pepper to taste
3 tablespoons chopped Italian parsley

SERVES 4

In a large, heavy skillet, heat the butter over medium heat. Add onion and cook until transparent, about 3–4 minutes. Gently toss with the cooked potatoes. Season with salt and pepper and fold in the parsley. Flatten slightly and cook until golden brown, about 3–4 minutes on each side.

Lyons, as the onion-growing region of France, places great emphasis on the use of onions in its cuisine. Any dish cooked "a la lyonnaise" is certain to include this versatile vegetable.

desserts

Strawberry Mousse in Flourless Pastry

Trattoria Dopo Teatro, courtesy of Roberto Lamorte

Butter for greasing
Flour for dusting
5 strawberries, cleaned and
  stems removed
2 cups heavy cream

5 eggs
½ cup sugar
Powdered sugar for garnish
Strawberries for garnish
Mint leaves for garnish

SERVES 4–6

Butter the bottom of an 8 x 13-inch jelly roll pan and cover with a sheet of parchment paper. Butter the parchment paper and lightly dust with flour. Set aside.

In a food processor, puree the strawberries. Add the heavy cream and process using the plastic blade until stiff peaks form and the mixture turns pink. Refrigerate.

Preheat oven to 500 degrees.

Put eggs and sugar in a large bowl and, using a hand mixer, beat until mixture doubles in size, about 6–8 minutes. Spread the mixture into the prepared pan and gently shake to distribute evenly. Bake for 2 minutes until golden and puffy. Cool completely. (The pastry will sink when it cools.) When the pastry has cooled, carefully remove it from the pan, leaving parchment paper intact. Evenly spread the mousse over the pastry. From the short end, roll the pastry into a log, removing the parchment paper as you go. Freeze the log for 15 minutes until firm enough to slice. Cut into 8–12 slices and allow mousse to soften a few minutes. Place 2 slices on each plate and garnish with a dust of powdered sugar, strawberries, and mint leaves.

{ This flourless dessert is light as air and sure to please at a springtime luncheon, tea, or brunch. }

Panna Cotta

Café Un Deux Trois, courtesy of Luis Gonzalez

½ cup passion fruit sorbet
6 gelatin sheets

2¼ cups heavy cream
1½ cups whole milk
¾ cup sugar

SERVES 6–8

Thaw the passion fruit sorbet to liquid but still cold. Break the gelatin sheets into the sorbet and let sit for 5 minutes. Bring the cream, milk, and sugar to a boil. Immediately remove from heat and cool in a cold water bath. Fold in the sorbet and gelatin blend and pour into ramekins.

Cover with plastic wrap and refrigerate for at least 12 hours. Serve with fresh fruit.

This satiny, rich custard, an Italian favorite, takes on a delightful twist with the addition of refreshing passion fruit sorbet. Served with your choice of fresh fruit, it is the perfect ending to any meal.

Brûlé, French for "to burn," is commonly associated with crème brûlée, the custard dessert with a crunchy, caramelized surface. The twist here is the addition of lemon juice and zest to give a delicious tart flavor.

Lemon Tart Brulée

Chez Josephine, courtesy of Frank Diaz

CRUST

1⅓ cups all-purpose flour

2 tablespoons sugar

2 teaspoons lemon zest

⅛ teaspoon salt

1 stick unsalted butter, cut
in ½-inch pieces

2–3 tablespoons ice water

FILLING

3 large eggs

½ cup plus 1 tablespoon sugar

⅓ cup whipping cream

⅓ cup fresh lemon juice

1 tablespoon lemon zest

Pinch of salt

SERVES 6–8

Preheat oven to 400 degrees.

Blend the flour, sugar, zest, and salt in a food processor.
Gradually add butter and pulse until it forms a coarse meal.
Drizzle in water until dough forms. Turn dough onto a work
surface, roll into a ball, and then flatten into a disc. Wrap in
plastic and refrigerate for 1 hour. Roll out on a lightly floured
work surface into a 13-inch round. Transfer to a 9-inch
tart pan with a removable bottom. Trim dough to a 1-inch
overhang. Fold overhang under, pressing to form a double-
thick edge. Freeze for 15 minutes. Bake in preheated oven until
pale golden brown, about 20 minutes. Set aside to cool.

In a bowl, whisk the eggs, ½ cup sugar, cream, lemon juice,
zest, and salt and blend well. Pour filling into cooled tart shell.
(Filling will not fill the shell). Bake until set, about 20–25
minutes. Cool completely.

Preheat the broiler.

Sprinkle remaining sugar over the tart. Cover sides of tart with
aluminum foil to prevent burning. Broil until sugar caramelizes
in spots, watching closely, about 3 minutes. Serve warm or at
room temperature.

Saintly Zeppoles

Patsy's, courtesy of Sal Scognamillo

2 cups water
1 tablespoon unsalted butter
2 pinches of salt
2 cups all-purpose flour

6 eggs
12 (3-inch) squares wax paper,
   lightly dusted with flour
Vegetable oil for frying

YIELDS 12

In a large, heavy saucepan, heat the water, butter, and salt over high heat to the boiling point. When boiling, gradually add flour and stir until thoroughly combined, about 1–2 minutes. Remove from heat, place in a mixing bowl and set aside to cool, about 10 minutes.

Adding one egg at a time, mix on low speed until each egg is incorporated. Place in a pastry bag and pipe out doughnut shapes onto each wax paper square.

Fried doughnuts, or fritters, are filled with ricotta cheese and chocolate chips to create an absolutely heavenly treat. They are also an important part of the Italian festival of San Guiseppe (St. Joseph) every March 19.

FILLING

2 pounds ricotta cheese

1½ cups granulated sugar

1 teaspoon vanilla extract

½ cup semisweet chocolate chips

Powdered sugar for dusting

12 maraschino cherries

In a large, deep skillet, heat 1-inch vegetable oil to 350 degrees. Carefully slide the doughnuts off the wax paper into the hot oil. Fry, turning often, until golden brown, about 6–8 minutes. When they double in size, remove from oil, drain, and allow to cool.

To make the filling, combine ricotta, sugar, and vanilla in a mixing bowl and mix with a hand mixer on medium speed for 2–3 minutes. Fold in the chocolate chips and mix an additional 10–15 seconds. Place the filling in a pastry bag. Cut each "doughnut" in half horizontally and fill the center with the cream filling. Gently press the top half onto the filling. Dust with powdered sugar and garnish each with a cherry.

"Recently, I was volunteer ushering at an Off Broadway show and the female lead was a well-known TV sitcom star. After seeing a great performance and picking up a few loose playbills, I bundled up for the cold winter night. Insulated in my coat, scarf, hat, and gloves, I opened the door to a crowded vestibule. Excited fans surged towards me, as I am of similar build as that actress. Startled at first, I realized who they thought I was. I smiled and muttered, 'I'm just the usher.' And continued into the night savoring my moment of fame."

—Linda Prickett, volunteer usher and writer

Tostadas de Vino

Sangria 46, courtesy of Benny Castro

1 (750 mL) bottle Tempanillo red wine
2½ cups sugar
1 loaf day-old French or Portuguese
   bread, cut into 2-inch slices

Unsalted butter
Vanilla ice cream

SERVES 4–6

In a saucepan, whisk together the wine and sugar and heat
until the sugar dissolves.

In a large serving dish, place the bread slices and cover with
the wine/sugar mixture. Place in the refrigerator for 20–25
minutes, turning the bread slices every 10–15 minutes.

In a large, heavy skillet, melt 1–2 tablespoons butter. Add
bread slices in batches and, over medium heat, brown about
2–3 minutes on each side. (Add more butter as needed.) Serve
warm with vanilla ice cream.

Tostadas de Vino is an old-world recipe using
yesterday's bread to create a simple, economi-
cal yet lovely and tasty dessert.

Manzanas al Horno

Meson Sevilla, courtesy of Joaquin Lucero

4 large baking apples (Rome
    Beauty or Golden Delicious)
4 cinnamon sticks
4 cups granulated sugar

4 cups dry white wine
Unsalted butter for greasing
Vanilla ice cream

SERVES 4

Preheat oven to 375 degrees.

Wash and core the apples, removing cores to ½ inch from the
bottoms. Scrape seeds out with a spoon. Grease a baking dish
with butter and place apples upright. Fill each apple with a
cinnamon stick, 1 cup sugar, and 1 cup wine. (There will be
overflow.) Bake for 30–40 minutes, or until apples are brown
and tender. Serve warm with vanilla ice cream.

{ The smell of apples and cinnamon is so much a
part of the feel of autumn. Simple ingredients
and simple baking make this an ideal treat to
take away fall's chill. }

Mascarpone, native to the Lombardy region of Italy, is a buttery, creamy, spreadable cheese that is perfectly paired with fruits.

Cheese and Cherry Blintzes

Russian Tea Room, courtesy of Petrous Moldovan

BLINTZES
¾ cup whole milk
½ cup blonde beer
6 eggs
3 tablespoons sugar
1 teaspoon salt
1⅓ cups flour
2 tablespoons melted butter, not hot

CHEESE FILLING
¾ cup cream cheese
¼ cup sour cream
¼ cup mascarpone
1 tablespoon sugar
1 teaspoon vanilla extract

CHERRY FILLING
1¼ pounds fresh cherries, pitted
½ cup sugar
1 teaspoon vanilla extract

SERVES 4

In a large bowl, thoroughly combine the milk, beer, eggs, sugar, and salt. Place the flour in another large bowl and form a well in the center. Gradually add the liquid mixture and whisk slowly until all is incorporated. Place in a blender, add the butter and blend until smooth. Heat a crêpe pan over medium heat. Add 2–3 tablespoons batter and swirl to coat bottom of pan. Cook until lightly browned, about 1–2 minutes on one side and 1 minute on other side. (You need 8 crêpes; this recipe makes more than 8, but the first few may not come out perfectly. Any extra crêpes can be wrapped in plastic and frozen.) When crêpes are cooked, lay them flat to cool while you make the filling.

With a hand mixer, thoroughly combine all of the cheese filling ingredients. Divide the filling among 4 crêpes, roll and refrigerate.

In a heavy saucepan, cook all of the cherry filling ingredients over low heat for 10 minutes. Taste and add more sugar if desired. Place in the refrigerator and chill for 1 hour. Divide the cherry filling among the 4 remaining crêpes and roll.

Preheat oven to 375 degrees.

Before serving, place blintzes on a baking sheet and heat in a 375-degree oven for 6 minutes.

Lemon Ricotta Torte

Patsy's, courtesy of Sal Scognamillo

1 (3-pound) container whole
  milk ricotta cheese
1⅔ cups sugar
3 extra large eggs
½ teaspoon vanilla extract

Zest and juice from 1 lemon
Unsalted butter for greasing
All-purpose flour for dusting
Fresh mint to garnish (optional)

SERVES 8

Preheat the oven to 400 degrees.

In a large mixing bowl, thoroughly combine the cheese, sugar, eggs, vanilla, zest, and lemon juice. Grease a 9-inch round baking pan and lightly dust with flour. Pour the mixture into the pan and level the top with a spatula. Make a 2-inch collar for the pan with a 6 x 12-inch piece of foil, folded in half lengthwise. Wrap the collar around the pan and secure with cooking twine. Bake on the bottom shelf of the oven for 55–60 minutes. Remove from oven, cool, and refrigerate 3–4 hours. Return to room temperature before serving. Garnish with fresh mint, if desired.

Ricotta, so popular in Italian cooking, is actually a whey by-product of provolone, mozzarella, and pecorino. It is often used in desserts because of its slightly sweet taste.

Brazilian Flan

Brazil Brazil, courtesy of Ernane Sardinha

1 cup sugar

2 tablespoons water

1 (13.5-ounce) can condensed milk

13.5 ounces whole milk (use condensed milk can to measure)

6–7 ounces heavy cream (fill condensed milk can halfway to measure)

3 whole eggs

Mint leaves and fresh fruit to garnish

SERVES 4–6

In a saucepan, heat the sugar and water over medium-high heat, stirring constantly with a wooden spoon. When sugar liquefies and turns a light amber color, about 8–10 minutes, pour into a 2-quart flan mold. Tilt until the caramel spreads evenly on the bottom of the mold. Set aside to cool.

In a blender, combine the condensed milk, whole milk, cream, and eggs and blend until smooth. Pour into the flan mold.

Preheat oven to 375 degrees.

Place the mold on a roasting pan and add boiling water to the pan halfway up the side of mold. (Be careful not to get water in the mold.) Bake for 40 minutes. Cool and refrigerate overnight. Garnish with fresh mint and fruit.

A rich custard of condensed milk and heavy cream is baked in a bain-marie. This water bath is the secret to keeping the delicate flan from curdling.

drinks

Matilda

Algonquin Hotel

1 1/2 ounces Absolut Mandarin Vodka
1/2 ounce fresh orange juice

1/4 ounce Cointreau
Champagne

Pour vodka, orange juice, and Cointreau into a chilled champagne glass. Fill with champagne.

South Side

"21" Club

2 ounces gin or white rum
1 tablespoon fresh mint leaves

2 teaspoons granulated sugar
Juice of 1 lemon

Pour all ingredients into a shaker with ice. Shake vigorously to bruise mint leaves. Strain into a chilled collins glass filled with ice.

Cosmopolitan

Frankie & Johnnie's Steakhouse

1 ounce Stoli Orange Vodka
1 ounce cranberry juice
¼ ounce Cointreau

¼ ounce fresh lime juice
Dash of grenadine
Orange zest to garnish

Pour all ingredients, except orange zest, into a shaker with ice. Shake vigorously and strain into a chilled martini glass. Sprinkle with orange zest.

From Russia with Love

Russian Tea Room

½ ounce Dark Godiva Chocolate Liqueur
½ ounce Chambord

Champagne
Cocoa nibs to garnish

Mix liqueur and Chambord in a chilled champagne glass. Fill with champagne and decorate with cocoa nibs.

"Bobby soxers screaming and fainting at the sight of Frank Sinatra entering the Paramount building in Times Square! The image lightens up the faces of both tourists and locals alike on our culinary walking tour. Half a century ago, the 'famous' restaurants dotted Times Square. Today, our strolling adventure delights everyone with the diversity of old and new restaurants as well as the history of the 'Crossroads of the World.'"

—Liz Young, tour company owner

Red Passion

Victor's Café

1½ ounces Absolut Mandarin Vodka
½ ounce Cointreau
½ ounce passion fruit extract
½ ounce fresh lime juice

½ ounce simple syrup
Dash of cranberry juice
Orange wedge to garnish

Pour all ingredients, except orange wedge, into a shaker with ice. Shake vigorously and strain into a chilled martini glass. Garnish with orange wedge.

Au Revoir

Le Petit Café Un Deux Trois

2 ounces vodka
¾ ounce Midori

¾ ounce Cointreau
½ ounce apple schnapps

Pour all ingredients into a shaker with ice. Shake vigorously and strain into a chilled martini glass.

Mango Lassi (Non-Alcoholic)

Purnima

3 cups plain yogurt
1 cup canned mango pulp
½ cup whole milk

½ cup water
¼ cup granulated sugar

SERVES 4–6

Combine all ingredients in a blender until frothy and well combined. Pour into glasses filled with ice.

Cadillac Margarita

Iguana

1½ ounces Patron Anejo Tequila
½ ounce Cointreau

½ ounce fresh lime juice
Lime wedge to garnish

Pour all ingredients, except lime wedge, into a shaker with ice. Shake vigorously and strain into a salt-rimmed margarita glass. Garnish with lime wedge.

Folies Bergere

Chez Josephine

1½ ounces raspberry vodka
½ ounce Chambord

½ ounce Triple Sec
1 ounce champagne

Pour vodka, Chambord, and Triple Sec into a shaker with ice.
Shake vigorously and strain into a chilled champagne glass.
Top with champagne.

Mojito Bordelaise

Maison

8 fresh mint leaves
2 ounces Lillet White
1 ounce simple syrup

¾ ounce fresh lemon juice
1½ ounces champagne
Mint sprig and orange wedge to garnish

In a shaker, Muddle the mint leaves. Add Lillet, simple syrup,
and lemon juice. Add ice, shake vigorously and strain into a
highball glass. Top with champagne. Garnish with mint sprig
and orange wedge.

Sangria

Meson Sevilla

1 McIntosh apple, cored and thinly sliced
1 Valencia orange, thinly sliced
1 lemon, thinly sliced
3 tablespoons fine sugar (or more to taste)

1½ ounces Spanish brandy
1½ ounces Triple Sec
4 cups non-dry red or white Spanish wine
1 cup club soda

SERVES 2-4

Place fruit in a large carafe or pitcher. Add sugar, brandy, and Triple Sec and macerate for 1 hour. Fill with ice and pour in the wine and club soda.

Concord Grape Martini

Lucille's Grill at B. B. King's

3 concord grapes
4 mint leaves

3½ ounces vodka
½ ounce verjus

With a mortar and pestle, crush the grapes and mint leaves. Remove and place in a chilled martini glass. Pour vodka and verjus into a shaker with ice. Shake vigorously and strain into the martini glass.

Rasputin

Russian Tea Room

2 ounces Russian vodka   1 1/2 ounces Frangelica

Pour into a rock glass with ice. Stir and serve.

Classic Martini

Sardi's

2 1/2 ounces gin   Green olives or lemon twist to garnish
1/2 ounce dry vermouth

Pour gin and vermouth into a shaker with ice. Shake vigorously
and strain into a chilled martini glass. Garnish with olives or
lemon twist.

Manhattan

Sardi's

1½ ounces bourbon whisky
2 dashes sweet vermouth

Dash of angostura bitters
1 maraschino cherry to garnish

Pour whisky, vermouth, and bitters into an old-fashioned glass filled with ice. Garnish with the cherry.

Moscow Mule

Russian Tea Room

2½ ounces Stoli vodka
1 ounce fresh ginger puree
½ ounce simple syrup

Dash of fresh lime juice
Dash of angostura bitters
Ginger ale

Pour all ingredients, except ginger ale, into a highball glass filled with ice. Top with ginger ale.

Sidecar Normand

Maison

Lemon wedge and sugar/cinnamon
   mix to garnish glass rim
1½ ounces Calvados Fine
¾ ounce fresh lemon juice

¾ ounce honey syrup (50 percent
   honey and 50 percent water)
¾ ounce Cointreau

Rub rim of martini glass with lemon wedge. Dip glass rim into the sugar/cinnamon mix. Pour Calvados, lemon juice, honey syrup, and Cointreau into a shaker with ice. Shake vigorously, strain, and pour into glass.

The Cavitini

Russian Tea Room

2 ounces Imperia vodka
2 green olives
1 slice cucumber (6 inches
   long and ¼ inch thick)

1 teaspoon Wild American
   Hackleback caviar

Pour vodka into a shaker with ice. Shake vigorously and strain into a chilled martini glass. Add olives. Place the cucumber slice across the glass and dollop with caviar.

Mango Mojito

Iguana

8 mint leaves
3 lime wedges
1 teaspoon sugar
2 ounces Don Q Puerto Rico Rum
1/2 ounce club soda

1/2 ounce 7UP
1/2 ounce sour mix
1/2 ounce mango puree
Sugar cane wedge and lime wedge
    to garnish

Muddle the mint leaves, lime wedges, and sugar in a shaker. Add all remaining ingredients, except the garnish, and some ice to the shaker. Shake vigorously and strain into a chilled highball glass filled with ice. Garnish with sugar cane and lime wedge.

restaurant directory

Algonquin Hotel
59 West 44th Street
212.840.6800
Pages 20, 47, 52, 97,
130, 154, 206

Basso56
2334 West 56th Street
212.265.2610
Pages 33, 61, 103

Bistecca Fiorentina
317 West 46th Street
212.258.3232
Pages 94, 149

Brazil Brazil
330 West 46th Street
212.957.4300
Pages 118, 126, 127,
133, 150, 203

Broadway Joe Steakhouse
315 West 46th Street
212.246.6513
Pages 19, 170

Café Un Deux Trois
123 West 44th Street
212.354.4148
Pages 57, 73, 74, 101,
107, 113, 191

Chez Josephine
424 West 43rd Street
212.594.1925
Pages 51, 102, 140, 155,
172, 174, 184, 193, 213

Ellen's Stardust Diner
1650 Broadway
212.956.5151
Pages 29, 53, 85, 117, 171

Frankie & Johnnie's
Steakhouse
269 West 45th Street
212.997.9494
Pages 48, 83, 179, 187, 207

Iguana
240 West 54th Street
212.765.5454
Pages 131, 161, 212, 218

Iridium
1650 Broadway
212.582.2121
Pages 45, 160

Joe Allen
326 West 46th Street
212.581.6464
Pages 40, 152, 175

La Rivista
313 West 46th
212.245.1707
Pages 67, 91, 141

Lattanzi
361 West 46th Street
212.315.0980
Pages 41, 81, 98

Le Petit Café Un
Deux Trois
403 West 43rd Street
212.489.4900
Pages 137, 211

Le Rivage
340 West 46th Street
212.765.7374
Pages 135, 143, 148, 186

Lucille's Grill at B.B. King
237 West 42nd Street
212.997.4144
Pages 36, 63, 136, 164, 167, 214

Maison
1700 Broadway
212.757.2233
Pages 31, 70, 166, 174, 213, 217

Market Diner
572 11th Avenue
212.244.2888
Pages 49, 55, 99

Meson Sevilla
344 West 46th Street
212.997.0521
Pages 21, 71, 111, 199, 214

Orso
322 West 46th Street
212.489.7212
Pages 90, 106, 220

Patsy's
236 West 56th Street
212.247.3491
Pages 24, 39, 42, 76,
95, 139, 194, 202

Pergola Des Artistes
252 West 46th Street
212.302.7500
Pages 18, 129, 146

P.J. Clarke's
44 West 63rd Street
212.957.9700
Page 183

Purnima
245 West 54th Street
212.307.9797
Pages 41, 114, 212

The Russian Tea Room
150 West 57th Street
212.581.7100
Pages 54, 82, 109, 125, 158,
201, 207, 215, 216, 217

Sangria 46
338 West 46th Street
212.581.8482
Pages 30, 32, 44, 157, 198

Sardi's
234 West 44th Street
212.221.5440
Pages 66, 122, 151, 171,
175, 177, 184, 215, 216

Trattoria Dopo Teatro
125 West 44th Street
212.869.2849
Pages 25, 89, 147, 190

'21' Club
21 West 52nd Street
212.582.7200
Pages 26, 79, 119

Victor's Café
236 West 52nd Street
212.586.7714
Pages 23, 60, 110, 211

index

Metric Conversion Chart

Volume Measurements		Weight Measurements		Temperature Conversion	
U.S.	Metric	U.S.	Metric	Fahrenheit	Celsius
1 teaspoon	5 ml	½ ounce	15 g	250	120
1 tablespoon	15 ml	1 ounce	30 g	300	150
¼ cup	60 ml	3 ounces	90 g	325	160
⅓ cup	75 ml	4 ounces	115 g	350	180
½ cup	125 ml	8 ounces	225 g	375	190
⅔ cup	150 ml	12 ounces	350 g	400	200
¾ cup	175 ml	1 pound	450 g	425	220
1 cup	250 ml	2¼ pounds	1 kg	450	230